CW00368985

POCKET
INFORMATION
TECHNOLOGY

POCKET
INFORMATION
TECHNOLOGY
JOHN BROWNING

The essentials of
information technology explained
from A to Z

THE ECONOMIST IN ASSOCIATION WITH
HAMISH HAMILTON LTD
Published by the Penguin Group
Penguin Books Ltd, 27 Wrights Lane, London W8 5TZ, England
Penguin Books USA Inc., 375 Hudson Street, New York,
New York 10014, USA
Penguin Books Australia Ltd, Ringwood, Victoria, Australia
Penguin Books Canada Ltd, 10 Alcorn Avenue, Toronto,
Ontario, Canada M4V 3B2
Penguin Books (NZ) Ltd, 182–190 Wairau Road, Auckland 10,
New Zealand

Penguin Books Ltd, Registered Offices:
Harmondsworth, Middlesex, England

First published by Hamish Hamilton Ltd
in association with
The Economist Books Ltd 1995

10 9 8 7 6 5 4 3 2 1

Printed in Great Britain by
William Clowes, Beccles and London
A CIP catalogue record for this book is available
from the British Library

ISBN 0-241-13472-2

CONTENTS

INTRODUCTION

Pocket Information Technology is one of a series of management titles that is designed to bring clarity to specialist subjects. It is written by John Browning, who was formerly a business, economics and technology correspondent with *The Economist*. He is now European Editor of *Wired* and a writer and consultant specialising in information technology. The book is divided into three parts.

Part 1 comprises essays on how companies are having to re-engineer themselves, the information highway, how increasingly intelligent machines will redefine the way in which people make decisions, and the threats to Microsoft's powerful position in the computer industry.

Part 2 is an A–Z of terms, acronyms and jargon such as Ada and Archie, MUD and MOO, Vapourware and Zeroth. In this section words in small capitals usually indicate a separate entry; however, all acronyms such as EU and TV are in small caps even if they have no separate entry.

Part 3 consists of several appendixes, including the world's largest IT suppliers, the growth in computers connected to the Internet, and a list of abbreviations and acronyms that appear in the book.

Other titles in the series are:

Pocket Accounting
Pocket Finance
Pocket Manager
Pocket Marketing
Pocket MBA
Pocket Negotiator
Pocket Strategy
Pocket Telecommunications

Part 1
ESSAYS

(Re) ENGINEERING A NEW CAPITALISM

"And now for something completely different." Monty Python's catchphrase is becoming a cliché in boardrooms around the world. Executives everywhere have seized upon the idea that technology can set them free from all the old rules and constraints of management. They have not yet entirely figured out what the new rules might be, but that has not prevented them from using technology to change everything anyway. The name for this managerial revolution is re-engineering.

Since 1990, when Michael Hammer published re-engineering's manifesto in the *Harvard Business Review* – in an article entitled "Don't Automate, Obliterate" – nearly all big companies, and most small ones, have embarked on at least one re-engineering project. By most estimates, about half of these efforts failed to reach their goals. Here lies the re-engineering dilemma. While it is obvious to any manager that new technology enables work to be organised very differently from the way it is organised today, there are as yet no hard and fast rules as to how the task should be approached, only compelling examples and a widespread sense of urgency.

Many executives will want to imitate Mervyn's, a middle-sized, middle-market chain of about 300 department stores spread across the USA. It added tens of millions of dollars a year to profits after spending nine months on re-engineering its inventory-control systems. By using computers to track sales more closely and to respond more quickly, it managed both to reduce inventory dramatically and to halve the frequency with which goods are out of stock when a customer asks for them.

Mervyn's is not alone. Banks, car-makers, insurance companies, retailers and a host of others can boast about inspiringly successful instances of re-engineering. But the big picture tells a different story. Despite the billions spent on putting computers on managers' desktops, growth in the overall productivity of the white-collar workers who use the machines has generally been disappointing. Underlying every re-engineering effort is the larger process of competitive markets groping towards a new equilibrium for economies dominated by trading in ideas rather than things, and powered by computers rather than motors.

Work harder, faster
Two factors are driving re-engineering. First, as most executives have already realised, computers and networks enable work to be done radically differently from how it was done before. Second, as they are now coming to realise, information, the raw material of today's service economies, is a different commodity, with different properties, from the iron and coal that fuelled the industrial revolution. These two factors rock the very foundations of industrial organisation.

One of the simplest and also most profound consequences of the new realities of capitalism is a shift from sequential processes to simultaneous ones. Information on a computer can be copied instantly and costlessly, so many people can work on the same thing at once, instead of passing it, step by time-consuming step, from one to another. This simple realisation is the source of some of the most impressive savings of re-engineering. IBM Credit, for example, used this insight to reduce the time needed to approve financial terms for the purchase of big computers – and thus to close the deal – from over a week to under four hours. Insurance companies have cut claims-processing times from weeks to minutes. But the new ways of working are not just faster, they are also fundamentally different.

Technology is breaking down the structures that separate companies from their customers. One of the first waves of disintermediation – that is, of removing middlemen from between buyer and seller – came in the 1970s, when people began getting their cash direct from a hole in the wall rather than from a teller. Then car-makers began placing orders directly into their suppliers' production-planning computers rather than picking from a warehouse, and Wal-Mart began stocking its shelves with Procter & Gamble goods directly from P&G's inventory, managed by P&G's computers, instead of via its own warehouses.

Further disintermediation will come with the growth of computer networks, like the Internet, which enable consumers to shop electronically both cheaply and easily. Companies that distribute goods over the Internet – like the Internet Shopping Network, which in 1994 was purchased by television's Home Shopping Network – have two big advantages over conventional mail-order. They need neither to print catalogues, because would-be customers browse their databases electronically, nor to employ banks of people to answer telephones, because customers place orders directly into the computers that fill them. Soon such disintermediation could affect everybody who makes their living from answering a telephone, from stockbrokers to warehouse staff. With change comes the necessity of learning new ways of working.

On the front line

As crumbling corporate structures put more and more workers on the front line of customer service, simply following established procedures is no longer good enough. Technology creates not just an opportunity for a transformation of work, but also the necessity to do so. Sharing information in databases makes it easier for everybody to see the big picture of the customer's problems, and thus to do the right thing rather than simply to follow the job description. But, as Tom Malone of the Massachusetts Institute of Technology (MIT) pointed out in a seminal article entitled "Electronic Markets and Electronic Hierarchies", published in the *Communications of the Association for Computing Machinery*, it also creates a managerial paradox.

At the simplest level, information technology makes it easier for firms to gather more information. To put that information to use, however, managers will want to use it to make decisions, which means turning more employees into decision-makers. And therein lies the rub. Traditional management involves telling people what to do. Yet the whole point of decision-makers is that they should decide for themselves what to do. Thus to persevere with a traditional managerial line of command is to waste most of the potential of new technology. But to eschew it is to step resolutely into a brave new managerial world.

Small, in the new world, is beautiful. Information work tends to lead to diseconomies of scale. While big factories may produce goods more cheaply than small ones, big committees tend to produce worse decisions, more expensively than small ones. Fred Brooks chronicled the phenomenon in his book *The Mythical Man Month*, an account of a huge, and hugely over-budget, software project undertaken at IBM in the late 1960s. Dr Brooks, who was managing the project, was shocked to find that adding more staff simply made the project fall further behind and become more expensive. The problem, he ultimately deduced, was that the extra time needed to co-ordinate a larger group of workers – to keep everybody up to speed on the underlying knowledge they needed to work together – quickly overwhelmed the extra contribution they could make to the project's success.

Although it is hard to assign cause and effect for changes that can be observed only through broad-brush statistics, similar forces could be reshaping the economy as a whole. In the USA, the UK and Germany the average size of firms began to fall in the early 1970s after nearly 200 years of steady growth. MIT's Erik Brynjolfsson further found that, industry sector by industry sector, declines in firm size were strongly correlated to investment in information technology. Even big firms are breaking down large bureaucracies in favour of smaller, often self-managing, teams. But in tapping the power of small groups, armed with computers, to outperform larger ones, companies fundamentally change the nature of management itself.

To function at the pace of today's highest-performing companies, managers must become coaches rather than commanders. There is simply no time to tell people what to do, or to check and cross-check work as it moves through a bureaucratic hierarchy. Instead, managers must increasingly focus on giving employees the background knowledge, the information and the resources to make decisions for themselves, preferably the right ones. This is, of course, easier said than done. It is one thing to recognise intellectually that real authority lies in the number of people who respect your ideas; it is another entirely to give up direct command over your department in the hope of leading by example and inspiration alone.

Golden rules

Given the scale of the changes that technology brings, it is no wonder that re-engineering is still a struggle. Nonetheless, three lessons have emerged which can help today's managers at least to struggle more productively than their predecessors.

1 Focus on results. By definition, re-engineering involves creating new ways of doing things. A crucial aid in that process of innovation is to focus on what needs to be done rather than the existing procedures for doing it; on creating demand rather than marketing; or on delivering goods on time rather than order-taking and inventory management. Focusing on results helps innovators to realise that some parts of their old procedures are no longer necessary, and that they can simplify dramatically.

2 Build technology infrastructure. The same technology which drives corporate change can also hinder it. Change in many firms is stymied by legacy systems which, by automating specific business procedures, have effectively cast them in electronic concrete. A better way, many companies find, is to try from the beginning to separate the generic functions that technology provides – like communications and databases – from the specific business logic of a given procedure. Companies like the Burlington Northern Railroad are demonstrating that, with some discrimination, it is possible to invest heavily in the former without committing to the latter. The infrastructure thus built can then provide a technical foundation on which re-engineering can happen fast.

3 Start as you would finish. One of biggest, and yet most understandable mistakes, which many re-engineering projects make, is to try to define carefully where they will end up before they begin. Re-engineering often creates such dramatic changes that it is impossible to imagine the details of work in the new world when the company sets forth from the old. When companies try to project ahead too carefully, they often end up with five-year plans which are irrelevant by the time they approach completion; and, worse, they create top-heavy planning bureaucracies in doing so. Mervyn's, by contrast, based its successful re-engineering of inventory management on a prototype which took two months to build, and another two months to prove its business value. Its basic value established, the system was improved steadily as it was rolled out, with suggestions based on use of the technology rather than theoretical hopes.

Despite all the frustration, the failures and the confusion of re-engineering, there is ample cause for optimism. As Paul David, an economic historian at Stanford University, has pointed out, industry often takes much longer than expected to pick up on new ways of working. At the end of the 19th century the advance of electricity made possible dramatically more productive factories, with individual motors at each workbench rather than a single, giant steam engine linked to workbenches by belts and pulleys. Proponents of the technology began proclaiming its virtues in about 1900, yet big productivity gains did not appear until the 1920s. So, as personal computers started becoming popular in the mid-1980s, the first decade of the 21st century could be a very good time indeed.

INFORMATION ROADWORK

The growth of the Internet has been one of the marvels of the late 20th century. By 1995 it linked some 5m computers around the world and, although estimates of its population are at best haphazard, probably over 30m people. It was still growing at 50-100% a year. Nobody is in charge. The Internet just grew, and in growing it inspired the much-hyped vision of the information super-highway: high-bandwidth communication links connecting people around the world, not to mention the schools, libraries, hospitals and offices they work in. Fulfilling that vision, however, inevitably promises to be a more fraught and com-plicated process than just inspiring it.

The Internet still falls far short of even the more realistic promises made for the information super-highway. It is merely popular, rather than ubiquit-ous. While fine for text and still pictures, its technology copes uncomfortably with live voice, interactive video and other information which must be received as quickly as it is sent. Designed for sharing information rather than securing it, the Internet's relative openness causes understand-able nervousness among those who would use it for commerce. There is a long way to go from Internet to I-way.

Whether the Internet evolves into a global information superhighway – or is replaced by something newer, more controllable and more commercial – rests ultimately on the answers to three questions: What do people want? What will governments let them have? What will companies find profitable to build? To understand the issues that will shape the growth of the information economy, start with the choices faced by con-sumers.

Getting wired
In 1995, at least, the easiest way to take a spin on the information superhighway was to sign up for an on-line service like CompuServe, America On-

Line or Delphi. Strictly, these are cyberspace's equivalent of shopping malls. They offer discussion groups, things to buy (mostly information) and some sort of – usually pretty limited – access to the broader Internet. About 7m Americans and 500,000 or so Europeans had signed up for on-line services by 1995.

For many, however, an increasingly attractive alternative was to connect directly to the Internet. Although often technically more challenging – particularly for the individual – a direct connection to the Internet typically offers more services at a lower price. One of the key advantages of a direct connection over a link via most on-line services is the opportunity to participate in the vast information bazaar growing up around a collection of software known as the World Wide Web.

The Web makes the global Internet almost as easy to use as Apple's Macintosh computer. Through hypertext, words and pictures are linked to other relevant words and pictures. So point the mouse, click and – whoosh – a computer thousands of miles away is telling you whatever you wanted to know. Between 1993 and 1995 tens of thousands of Web sites sprang up across the Internet. They created a sort of information market town, where anyone could be a producer, a consumer, or both. Among the stalls can be found information about BMW cars, industrial plastics from General Electric, Sony music, cross-dressing, legislation before the US Congress, logic programming and the personal tastes of Dan Bornstein (among thousands of other individuals who have made a personal statement on the Web).

The freedoms of the Web give small firms an unprecedented ability to compete with big ones. Roswell Computer Books reaches world markets from Halifax, Nova Scotia. Chris Cooper, a Californian entrepreneur, sells financial information in partial competition with Reuters and Dow Jones. Yet thanks to the Internet he can reach a larger market with an investment of a few hundred thousand dollars than his competitors do with proprietary networks costing millions.

Ultimately, however, both the rapid growth of the Internet and the freedom it provides rely on the fact that it offers consumers a choice. This is do-it-yourself infrastructure. Those who do not like the offerings of on-line service providers can relatively easily create their own. Big telephone companies provide only the bulk transmission capacity; the intelligence that makes the Internet interesting to use is provided by computers owned by customers themselves. That network intelligence can evolve as rapidly as customers want it to. Judging by the meteoric growth of the Web, which came from nowhere in 1993 to become the second-largest source of Internet traffic in 1995, that evolution can be very fast indeed.

The next generation

For all today's freedom and breakneck growth, a challenge looms just over the horizon that could change dramatically both the services the information superhighway offers and the way in which they are developed. That challenge is video. The ability to transmit video creates exciting new possibilities: videoconferencing instead of telephone calls; interactive video entertainment; better remote medical diagnosis and practice. The snag with video is that it requires higher communications bandwidth than today's infrastructure can easily provide. Companies looking to invest billions in new infrastructure quite understandably want assurances that they will receive some return on that investment. But in seeking such assurances they inevitably threaten to undermine the consumer choice that has made the development of the Internet so quick, so fruitful and so fundamentally democratic.

Ultimately it is governments that will have the biggest say in deciding who builds the next generation of infrastructure, and on what terms. For governments write the regulations that control telecoms markets. Unfortunately for those looking for a clear vision of the future of information superhighways to match politicians' bold promises to support it, governments are feeling deeply schizophrenic. They hope that, in the long term, unfettered competition will bring to telecoms markets the same relentless pressures to improve price and performance that have put ever cheaper and more powerful personal computers on every desktop. They have good reason. In the relatively deregulated USA most companies pay only about 15% of turnover for telecoms services, while in still-regulated Europe that figure can be as high as 30%. But, even as they strive to deregulate for the long term, over the short term governments want to regulate competition precisely to ensure that it may someday be unregulated. If you think that sounds like a difficult balancing act, you are right.

Russ Neuman of the Media Lab at the Massachusetts Institute of Technology predicts that soon most citizens of the developed world could face a choice of up to five competing telecoms networks: one evolved from the existing telephone network; another evolved from the existing cable-television network; a third evolved from the electricity network; a new fourth network which transmits over fixed radio links; and, finally, several competing services which offer mobile communications links (for a phone in every pocket). In the UK, at least, companies representing all of Mr Neuman's five sorts of competitor have already begun selling telecoms services, although some as yet compete only in limited markets.

Yet the UK government, like all governments deregulating telecoms, attributes growing competition to a system of checks and balances based on regulating both access to telecoms services and service provision itself. Access regulations are designed to prevent entrenched ex-monopolies from using their market power to crush competition. Should BT or Bell Atlantic prevent other companies from using their wires and infrastructure, any potential competitor would have to string up its own wires. Few would do that, so governments force former monopolies to offer new competitors the right to use their infrastructure at a price set by regulators. Similarly regulators ensure that cable-television companies offer more or less equal access to their wires for makers of television shows. They also ban telephone companies from competing with cable-television providers in the hope of providing sufficient security for cable firms to inspire them to build infrastructure that will someday compete with that created by the telephone companies.

Service regulation works on the other side of the fence. In order to make basic telephone service affordable for all, politicians have long encouraged – and in many cases required – telephone companies to keep prices low for "essential" basic services, like a telephone at home to make local calls. This is done by cross-subsidising these services from the high prices charged on advanced services, like long-distance calls or high-bandwidth data lines.

Marrying access and service regulations with governments' new-found desire for competition and innovation will be no mean feat. BT says that it would be happy to invest over £15 billion to bring fibre-optic cable to every home and office in the UK if it is allowed to carry television signals as well as voice and data. Regulators, fearing that this freedom will simply allow BT to trample fledgling cable companies – and thus to create not just a telephone monopoly but an information monopoly as well – have refused that permission until at least 1998, and probably later.

In the USA as much as $20 billion a year in cross-subsidies flows from long-distance and other advanced services to basic residential telephones. Needless to say, arguments over which services should be taxed, and which should be cheap, lie at the heart of the USA's debate over telecoms reform. The problem, of course, is that such schemes inevitably end up taxing the very advanced services they would promote for the information superhighway.

Coming attractions
Regulation, however, is only part of the uncertainty facing the telecoms giants trying to swing

into the fast lane of the information superhighway. There is also the problem of figuring out what customers will buy. All big telecoms companies want to provide fancy, advanced services rather than raw transmission capacity, if only because the profit margins are higher. But they do not yet seem to know what their customers really want.

Every big telephone company, and most big computer companies, have joined consortia hoping to create customised, global networks to manage the telecoms needs of giant corporations. In theory, the market could be worth billions of dollars a year. But, despite much effort, executives of would-be customers still complain that none of the giants has yet put together a collection of services that meets their needs.

As with big corporations, so too with consumers. In both the USA and the UK, cable companies and telephone giants have joined to try out interactive television services. Video on demand sends whatever movie you want to watch down the telephone line whenever you want to watch it. Interactive television allows people to play along with game shows from home. Some trials have also offered videoconferencing and computer-networking. But none of the services has yet caught the popular imagination. As video entertainment, they offer little that cannot be had with cable television and a local video-rental shop. In information retrieval and communications, they lag far behind the World Wide Web and the Internet.

Everywhere the gaps between the traditions of big telecoms and television companies and the challenges of the interactive future are many and huge. Charging by the minute for a connection, long the tradition in voice telephony, makes little sense for data networks. Here information is typically divided into packets, each of which may travel across the network using a different path, and at a different speed. Similarly advertising, which has long paid the bills of broadcast television, fits uneasily into a world of interactive video where consumers actively choose what to watch rather than absorbing what is on.

Given all the uncertainty, progress down the information superhighway is likely to be slow and bumpy – a far cry from the streamlined ride that politicians now promise. Indeed, uncertainty itself may play a key role in determining both the development of the I-way and its eventual shape. For an uncertain environment is best suited to small-scale local experimentation, to people creating for themselves what they want rather than waiting for big business to give it to them. This is how the Internet grew – and how it is growing still. After all, there can be no better way to ensure that people get the future they want than to enable them to build it for themselves.

INVASION OF THE MIND SNATCHERS

For at least as long as they have used computers, people have been scared of them. Inasmuch as these machines can reason – not very much at present but improving all the time – they threaten to duplicate the very intelligence that sets people apart from animals. So neo-Luddites accuse them of destroying jobs and science-fiction writers dream up artificial intelligences that want to take over the world. While perhaps understandable, these fears are misplaced. Computers are neither technically nor economically suited to usurp human beings' place at the centre of their own universe. But what they are doing is, if less serious, far more uncomfortable: they are forcing people to re-evaluate their skills. Whole people are not being made redundant, but parts of them are.

More jobs, different jobs

During the next decade or two one of the most intriguing tasks facing people in developed economies will be to find ways of living with the new reasoning powers of their creations. It is hogwash to argue that computers destroy jobs. In the USA, which is probably the world's most heavily automated economy, the proportion of the human population employed has risen steadily alongside the population of computers. In 1950, when 105m Americans might possibly have found paid employment, 56% did so. In 1970, 57% of a possible 137m were in paid employment. By 1990, however, with the entry of more and more women into the workforce 63% of a possible 188m worked for money. But computers do change jobs since it is seldom worth paying a person to undertake a task that can easily be done by machine. So the challenge for bosses and workers alike is to create combinations of men and machines whose capabilities are greater than the sum of the parts.

A brief glance at the history of computers in medical diagnosis shows some of the opportunities and problems. Since the late 1960s, when Edward Shortliffe at Stanford University created MYCIN, the first medical expert system, computers have on average been able to out-diagnose human doctors in their mutual specialities. For doctors who have devoted years of study to learning diagnostic skills, this is embarrassing. But it does not threaten their livelihoods. In the few instances where computers fail, they do so spectacularly – and it is no good being a bit better on 98% of patients if the machine idiotically kills the remaining 2%.

While computers cannot be trusted to practise medicine on their own, neither can they work with people. Only doctors have the knowledge to engage in a fruitful dialogue with a medical expert system, but they do not have the time to do so. It simply takes too long for a doctor to type the necessary information into the machine. Researchers have a variety of ideas for making diagnostic expert systems more useful. Some want to integrate them into the computer systems which handle patient records, so that they can automatically make suggestions for treatment. Some reckon that patients should work with the systems directly, which would provide them with advice the doctor might be too busy to give and enable them to gather material to provide the doctor with a succinct briefing. Others hope that better computer interfaces, perhaps using voice or graphics, will speed communication between doctor and machine.

Can they be one of us?

In the face of such problems, some researchers in artificial intelligence still dream of bridging the gap between intelligent man and increasingly intelligent machines by making the two more or less indistinguishable. One of most popular tests of computer intelligence – the Turing Test, named after a British computer pioneer, Alan Turing, who proposed it – posits that a computer can only be considered intelligent if it can trick humans into thinking it is one of them over the course of a brief conversation. No computer can do that; nor is one likely to do so for the foreseeable future. But that does not make them useless. On the contrary, many of the most useful machines have only an idiot-savant's snippet of intelligence. They thrive on the ability to do one very narrow reasoning task very well.

Some of the not-so-intelligent capabilities which enable machines to make smart decisions include the following.

- The ability to search rapidly through millions of possibilities. Computers regularly beat humans at chess armed with no more than the ability to look at a few million possible combinations of moves and choose the best. They also help airlines schedule maintenance and crews for their jets, and they determine the most efficient sequence of production in factories.
- The ability to apply a few rules thoroughly and relentlessly to the information at hand. Expert systems consist of a handful of rules in the form of "if such-and-such, then so-and-so". Embedded in corporate help desks – that is, the centres where the problems of frustrated customers are sorted out – they recommend who in the corporate bureaucracy can best solve the problem at hand. Embedded in word processors, they help recommend attractive ways to format a document.
- The ability to recognise patterns. Neural nets mimic the pattern-recognition machinery which nature evolved in humans; that is, the nerve cells in the brain, the eyes and other sense organs. They are being used to scan patterns of credit-card transactions to ferret out fraud, or, linked to video cameras, for quality inspection on production lines.
- The ability to remember perfectly. Some companies store their collective experiences using so-called case-based reasoning. When employees encounter a situation they are unsure of how to deal with, they can ask the computer to see if any of their colleagues dealt with a similar

situation before, and to find out how they did so. Equally, researchers at MIT are working on techniques that might enable computers to make helpful suggestions by noting things which other colleagues in similar jobs are doing, but which they are not.

Agents of influence

Realising the usefulness of these narrow abilities, researchers in artificial intelligence are turning their attention from creating artificial people to creating agents. Like helpful insects, each agent makes itself useful by doing a single, simple task, automatically, at its master's bidding. Given a bit of pattern-recognition and a dash of rule-application, for example, an agent might search computer networks for the most convenient flight for its master's holiday, or select possibly romantic destinations. But to take advantage of agents, people's own jobs may change dramatically.

At First Direct, a British bank that does its business by telephone, computers examine the recent transactions of each customer on the line. Using rules of thumb and statistics, the machines predict financial services that the customer might want to buy, and plant that idea on the screen of the relevant salesperson. For salespeople who delight in recognising the patterns that foretell what a customer might want to buy next, this is an intrusion which deadens their joy in their work. For salespeople who enjoy the patter, the conversation of selling, it can be a liberation. In practice, adding a bit of extra intelligence splits apart sets of skills that may never before have been separated.

The collective subconscious

As machines get smarter, it is not just individuals who must cope with an influx of new skills brought into the office on silicon. The same problems and opportunities apply to groups. Unlike traditional decision-making, First Direct's approach to handling customers was neither learned nor evolved via trial and error. It was purchased from a small software company called

Third Wave. As such companies learn to capture decision-making skills and embed them in software, some previously valuable skills may become over-the-counter commodities. Indeed, many American taxpayers already buy their tax accountant on a disk, in the form of the expert systems embedded in popular tax-preparation programs like Turbo Tax.

While an off-the-shelf accountant is undeniably convenient, skills purchased in a box do not evolve like those carried in people. The accountants who provide the expertise embodied in the software do not talk directly to the people using it. They may lose touch with their problems. Equally, however good the software is at answering clients' questions, it will not be as good as a person in prompting them to ask questions they would not otherwise have thought of. Even if the software does manage to capture all of the skills of a good tax accountant – and, helpful though today's products are, none yet really comes close – it still does not fully participate in the social conversations through which humans learn, and inspire each other to learn.

For there is still a great difference between providing tax advice and being a human being. One of the ironies of artificial intelligence is that computers' fast-increasing skill in solving intellectual problems – like playing chess or giving tax advice – only highlights their complete failure to cope with common-sense problems like understanding a children's story or playing a video game. As Terry Winograd, an artificial-intelligence researcher and sceptic at Stanford University, has pointed out, being a human requires a lot of experience and a lot of shared assumptions. It requires knowing about hunger, forgetting, boredom and being in a body, and all the other things learned when growing up.

Recreating all of that human knowledge, not to mention the decision-making machinery that brings it to life, is hard. While it is probably the most fascinating research project conceivable, it may also turn out to be one with surprisingly little practical value. The whole point of putting machines to work as decision-makers is that they do not act like people. They do not forget. They do not get bored. They do not get surly. They are alien.

If what people really want is something that makes decisions just like a person, then there are plenty of real people about. Should shortages arise, there are well-known techniques for creating more, which employ a minimum of technology and are likely to bear results long before artificial intelligence succeeds in recreating people from machines. But if what they really want is better decisions, then they had better learn to work with smart machines, however alien and irritating they may be.

LEADERS OF THE PACK

Some companies achieve greatness; others have greatness thrust upon them. Each in its own era, both IBM and Microsoft have managed both. For in the computer industry, success breeds success. The popularity of technologies developed by IBM and Microsoft increased their power to set future technological standards, and so set the course of competition in a direction which favoured their own products. Although both firms have been extensively investigated by the USA's Justice Department for allegedly anti-competitive practices, no serious charges were brought against either. Given the industry's history, two questions dominate discussions of the future of computer markets. Who, if anyone, will next wield the sorts of powers held by IBM and Microsoft? Or, in a maturing computer market, will this sort of power become as obsolete as the vacuum tube?

Elements of success

Although IBM and Microsoft came to prominence in different eras and with different technologies, many basic elements of their success stories are the same. In 1965 IBM shipped the first of its System 360 range of mainframe computers. Not only was the 360 based on the then new technology of integrated circuits, but it was also the first family of computers to offer companies a chance to upgrade from small entry-level machines to more powerful ones, as their computing needs grew, without changing their software.

Microsoft got its chance to shine in 1981, when its DOS operating system was offered by IBM on its first personal computer. Unusually for IBM, in its haste to get a personal computer to market, it did not acquire exclusive rights to either DOS or the Intel microprocessor which powered its computer. Yet with the reassuring bulk of IBM behind them, both technologies quickly became *de facto* standards in the marketplace. In the 16 months after the launch of the IBM personal computer,

Microsoft licensed DOS to 50 other computer-makers.

For both IBM in 1965 and Microsoft in 1981, an initial lead on the competition launched them into a self-reinforcing cycle of success. Part of that self-reinforcement came from customers' fears. In the fast-moving world of technology, even know-ledgeable customers can make expensive mis-takes. So, if all else fails, buying the most popular brand means that you are no more embarrassed than most other people. (Or, to put it more suc-cinctly: "Nobody ever got fired for buying IBM.")

But there is a stronger reason for going with the majority: protecting investments made in soft-ware. Because IBM and Microsoft held the largest market share, more developers of commercial software created products for their computers than for rivals. The availability of software, in turn, increases the value of the computers it runs on, which helps to inspire more software, and so on. A steady flow of software innovation, in turn, helps to convince companies that data which can only be accessed using some particular kind of software will continue to be accessible via such software.

IBM's fall

IBM fell from grace largely because it underestim-ated both the personal computer in general and the power of the forces which its own personal computer had set in motion. In the USA, at least, sales of personal computers grew at about 22% a year through the 1980s, to about $25 billion in 1994, while sales of mainframes grew at only about 4% a year, to $16 billion. This created a conundrum for IBM. Even today, mainframe com-puters account for nearly half of IBM's revenues, and by far the most profitable half. Mainframe cus-tomers require a lot of services, all of which they pay for, and IBM can hold its mainframe customers tight within the embrace of its proprietary tech-nical architecture. Yet the mainframe market was stagnating. So throughout the 1980s IBM kept try-ing, and failing, to innovate its way back to into the driver's seat in personal computers as well as mainframes.

Part of IBM's problem was simply that its products were expensive, the legacy of the high corporate overheads developed to provide a handholding service to mainframe customers. But the larger, more subtle problem for IBM was simply that its potential customers did not trust it. They feared that IBM would do what was good for IBM, not for its customers. Competitive personal computer markets – where any number of vendors could buy Intel chips and Microsoft operating systems to build computers compatible with the technical standards set by IBM – offered freedom as well as low prices. IBM tried to woo customers back into its fold with new lines of personal computers, which contained proprietary technologies. Customers resisted. But the final straw came with IBM's break with Microsoft over operating-system strategy.

Although IBM and Microsoft developed OS/2 jointly as the successor to DOS, the two gradually split over strategy. IBM felt its customers wanted the advanced features of OS/2. Microsoft thought that most computer users were not ready and would prefer Windows, which was less technically ambitious but required less computing muscle and technical expertise to run. By 1992 IBM and Microsoft were in competition, and Microsoft won. In that year IBM sold 1m copies of OS/2, while Microsoft sold 10m copies of Windows. As it is the software of operating systems that increasingly determines what computers can and cannot do, this victory has left Microsoft as the company most likely to dictate the direction of the next steps in the personal computer revolution.

The Microsoft challenge
Microsoft's challenge has three parts:

- to continue to dominate the market for desktop operating systems;
- to expand further its healthily growing sales of word processors, spreadsheets and other appli-

cations software;
- to move into the new markets being opened up by networks and other new media.

It is the third challenge which will be most important for Microsoft's future growth, for personal computer markets are reaching saturation point. But it is in expanding on to networks that Microsoft most runs the risk of being hoist with its own competitive petard.

Microsoft's most important venture into networking markets is the Microsoft Network. This on-line service will provide both a kind of electronic library-cum-shopping mall and links to the larger Internet. The capability to link into the network comes with Microsoft's next-generation Windows 95 operating system, which gives the Microsoft Network a potential membership several times larger than any other on-line service. But as it moves on to networks, Microsoft must increasingly face some of the same market forces with which it dethroned IBM.

Microsoft did not create the technologies of the Internet. It must therefore develop its own strategy to cope with technical standards set by others, and it must do this in markets which are increasingly suspicious of Microsoft's market power. As computer buyers become more knowledgeable this will become more difficult. Microsoft justifies the fees charged for Microsoft Network by arguing that it is much easier to use than the Internet. But as customers become more sophisticated and Internet support becomes more widespread, such a premium may come to seem as anachronistic as that which IBM tried to charge for its personal computers.

Competition is hotting up
Microsoft must compete with firms which are getting better at the game of innovating in the face of entrenched competitors. Microsoft prospered by making its operating systems cheap and widely available. To jump-start their own markets, other firms are distributing their wares for free. A prod-

uct called Acrobat, from Adobe, illustrates the problems and the opportunities of networked markets.

Acrobat is designed to enable electronic distribution of text and graphics across machines so different that they would not normally be able to display images that looked even vaguely similar. This is a potentially valuable service. The snag is that nobody is going to distribute text or graphics in Adobe's format until there is a lot of software out there to view them, and nobody is going to want the software until there are a lot of text and graphics to view. So, after trying unsuccessfully to sell the viewer software, Adobe began simply giving it away, in the hope of jump-starting a larger market for the technology. Similarly Netscape, a Silicon Valley start-up, gave away its eponymous World Wide Web browser in the hope of jump-starting a market for software to create the servers which provide information to those browsers.

Slowly, piece by piece, such competitors promise to chip away at Microsoft's market power just as Microsoft itself eroded IBM's. Microsoft may yet prove to be the last leader of the computer pack. Not because its power will last forever because it will not, but because after Microsoft a combination of maturity and the new capabilities of networks may make computer markets more diverse. Instead of one dominant leader, many lesser ones may develop.

Given enough computing power and communications bandwidth, it is possible largely to break free of the limitations of proprietary technologies. The Internet is composed of a variety of networks employing a variety of different networking technologies. They are linked by bridges which translate messages from one into a format that can be understood by another. Similarly computers from both Apple and Sun Microsystems now mimic Microsoft's Windows operating system sufficiently well to run many Windows programs. Such translations and emulations are never as good as the real thing, but they are steadily making it easier to switch from one technology to another.

As the costs of guessing wrong decrease, computer buyers should be more willing to experiment. Similarly, given the size of today's mature computer markets, it is increasingly hard to justify rationally the widespread belief that the only computer markets worth competing for are those created by the dominant technological standard. Although new technologies will still be dominated by the quickest innovators – and those who have managed to jump on their bandwagon – the mainstream should relax into diversity. The king is dying. Long live the kings to come.

Part 2

A–Z

ABDUCTION

A form of reasoning which derives premises from conclusions. For example, if you know that "if it rains, then the ground is wet" you could use DEDUCTION to conclude that the ground is wet from the knowledge that it rains, but you could abduce that it rains from the knowledge that the ground is wet. People use abduction all the time, but it is not, as logicians love to point out, logically sound. The relation between premise and conclusion is looser than vice versa. Although it is certain that rain will wet the ground, there could be other reasons why the ground is wet: because of a sprinkler, for example, or flooding.

ACK

Short for acknowledgement. It symbolises a code sent in many communications protocols to denote that the recipient has received and understood the message. (Contrast to NACK.)

ADA

The programming language used for most projects undertaken for the USA's Department of Defense. It was named after Ada Lovelace, daughter of Lord Byron, who became the world's first computer programmer when she helped Charles Babbage to construct his "difference engine", a computer made of brass gears and cogs, in the 1840s. The lady was reputed to be elegant; the language was designed by a military-industrial committee.

Charles Babbage's difference engine, designed between 1847 and 1849, had 4,000 parts. It weighed about 3 tons, and was 7 feet high and 11 feet long. It was never completed.

ADSL

Short for Asynchronous Digital Subscriber Loop, a proposed technology for sending video and other high-BANDWIDTH DATA over the existing copper wires running to homes and businesses, without investing billions in upgrading basic infrastructure to FIBRE OPTIC. ADSL assumes that most homes and businesses will consume far more data than they produce. So while it manages to send up to about 1.5m BITS of INFORMATION a second into the home, it does so by restricting the amount that can be sent back in the other direction. This makes ADSL suitable for showing movies, but not for video-conferencing.

AGENT

A much-ballyhooed piece of SOFTWARE that will do its master's bidding without direct supervision, even remotely, over a NETWORK. For example, an agent will find travel information without requiring its owner to know anything about electronic AIRLINE RESERVATION SYSTEMS. In practice this is easier marketed than done.

AI

See ARTIFICIAL INTELLIGENCE.

AIRLINE RESERVATION SYSTEMS

The first computer systems in business which not only improved efficiency, but also provided a tighter grip on customers. In the late 1980s airline reservation systems gained the distinction of being the first computer systems to be regulated under US anti-trust law. Their history provides an intriguing study of the changing role of information technology in business.

The first airline reservation system was created jointly by American Airlines and IBM in the 1960s to increase the efficiency with which American could track its highly perishable inventory of seats. American quickly realised that, if it could put its reservation terminals on to the desks of travel agents, it could capture an exclusive distribution channel. But so did other airlines, notably United, which began to compete for the privilege of wiring travel agents. Travel agents, in turn, played one airline off against another, and accepted those terminals which offered them access to the broadest range of flights for least money.

Instead of exclusivity, airlines consoled themselves with marketing bias: presenting their flights first in the list, for example, or making reservations on other carriers harder to confirm. At this point, after complaints from airlines which had not developed their own reservation systems, US federal regulators promulgated strict rules governing bias in the presentation of reservations information.

Meanwhile, with the advent of price and route deregulation in the 1970s, airlines began mining their reservations systems for the market information needed to construct increasingly elaborate pricing structures with more and more special fares, each aimed at a smaller subsection of the flying public. Today the big airline reservation systems – notably American Airlines' Sabre and United's Apollo – are run as arm's length subsidiaries, charging set fees for each reservation made or piece of marketing information accessed. In some years they have made more money than the airlines which spawned them.

A-LIFE
See ARTIFICIAL LIFE.

ALGORITHM
A step-by-step recipe for performing some calculation or decision process; what computer programs are made of.

ALPHA
Preliminary version of SOFTWARE or HARDWARE, a working prototype. It is buggier and more preliminary even than BETA.

AMERICAN STANDARD CODE FOR INFORMATION INTERCHANGE
See ASCII.

AMPLITUDE
The strength of a communications signal, which is easiest to visualise as the height of the electromagnetic wave.

Figure 1 **Analog and digital signals**

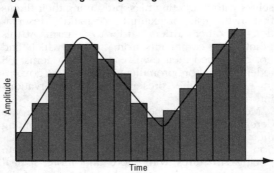

Amplitude

Time

ANALOGUE

Describes a signal which varies smoothly and continuously over time, as opposed to DIGITAL, which describes a signal encoded as a sequence of on-or-off, one-or-zero, BITS. Analogue signals are capable of more subtle and faithful reproduction than digital, particularly for music, voice or other signals which naturally vary smoothly and continuously. They are also, however, harder to transmit and to reproduce. Digital signals can be reproduced perfectly through the use of error correction. Analogue signals cannot; they suffer from NOISE and degradation.

To take advantage of the best qualities of both digital and analogue, many machines convert between the two. Compact disks, for example, store digitally encoded music and convert it to an analogue signal to be sent to the speakers. Telephone systems increasingly transmit digital signals and convert to and from analogue at earpiece or receiver.

One way of doing this is to convert at some point the strength, or AMPLITUDE, of the analogue signal into a BINARY number, and vice versa. The problem, however, is that these binary approximations themselves take time to create and to transmit, while the original analogue signal varies continuously. So the process is much like trying to reproduce the flow of a curve with a collection of rectangles (see Figure 1). The height of the rectangle represents the amplitude of the signal, while the width represents the time needed to transmit the digital number. Much effort and technology has been devoted to "blurring" digital signals into realistic and accurate analogue ones.

AND

Describes an operation in BOOLEAN ALGEBRA, often embodied as an electronic circuit, which returns 1 (or on) if, and only if, all of its inputs are 1 (or on). Otherwise it returns 0 (or off).

ANTI-VIRAL

A program that can detect, and sometimes eliminate, computer viruses.

Steve Wozniak sold his prize possession to finance development of the Apple I computer: his Hewlett Packard calculator. Steve Jobs sold his VW minibus.

APPLE

The company that invented the first commercially successful PERSONAL COMPUTER (PC). In 1976 Steve Jobs and Steve Wozniak began building Apple I computers in the garage of Mr Jobs's parents' home in Cupertino, California, and selling them to fellow computer hobbyists for $666 apiece. Their next model, the Apple II, launched in 1977, was the first PC to sell beyond the hobbyist market. By 1981 its success had inspired IBM to create its own rival PC, and Apple's fortunes began a long and largely self-inflicted decline.

Apple's answer to IBM's PC was the MACINTOSH, launched in 1984 amid growing corporate strife that in 1985 saw Mr Jobs ousted by John Sculley, who Mr Jobs had recruited from soft-drinks-maker Pepsi to bring experienced management to his fledgling firm. The Macintosh was a technological marvel. Its GUI set standards for ease of use that rivals spent a decade striving to emulate. But SOFT-

WARE for the run-of-the-mill tasks like word processing was scarce, and Mr Sculley's insistence on high profit margins kept prices high. Apple's market share shrank steadily through the 1980s. Mr Sculley was himself ousted in 1993, after disappointing initial sales of the product he had championed as Apple's next great gadget, the Newton PDA, or personal digital assistant. Macintosh prices were cut and market share recovered, but Apple still seems likely to go down in the history of the computer as the great might have been.

> *To correct a manufacturing error, Apple recommended to buyers of the Apple III computer that they lift the machine a couple of feet from a hard surface and drop it.*

APPLETALK
APPLE'S proprietary technology for creating local area networks with MACINTOSH computers. The company has recently released a faster version of Appletalk, called ETHERTALK, for use on ETHERNET networks

APPLICATION
Describes a WORD PROCESSOR, SPREADSHEET, accounting program or other piece of SOFTWARE which does useful work directly for the end user. SYSTEMS SOFTWARE, by contrast, includes programming languages, OPERATING SYSTEMS and other things needed to build and to run applications software.

APPLICATION LAYER
That part of the SEVEN LAYER REFERENCE MODEL which concerns the formatting of DATA on the screen, the proper conventions for FILE names and other aspects of translating from the technical conventions of one computer system to those of another, on the other side of the NETWORK.

ARCHIE
A tool for locating SOFTWARE and technical INFORMATION on the INTERNET. Over the years the Internet

has accumulated vast resources of computer software. After all, this is where researchers and students share their ideas for new technologies and hackers vie with each other to show who can write the coolest code. The problem was that finding what you wanted could sometimes be more trouble than writing the program again from scratch, at least until Archie came along. It searches for software by name across the NETWORK and then reports what is where.

ARPANET
Grandfather of many of today's large-scale computer networks, particularly the INTERNET. The Arpanet began in 1969 as a research project led by the Defence Advanced Research Projects Agency, from whose acronym, DARPA, the NETWORK derived its name. The goal was to create a computer network capable of supporting the USA's defence through a nuclear war. This meant that the network could not have a central switch or authority which could be pre-emptively destroyed. Taken together with the decision to encourage the researchers building the network to use it to share INFORMATION, this lack of central structure meant that the Arpanet could, and did, evolve into more or less whatever size and shape its denizens desired; in this case, the Internet.

The techniques of artificial intelligence are to the mind what bureaucracy is to human social interaction.
Terry Winograd

ARTIFICIAL INTELLIGENCE
The quest to make machines that can think as intelligently as people. Conceived in the mid-1950s, artificial intelligence (AI) raised high hopes when computers began to make relatively rapid progress in solving LOGIC problems and learning to play chess. Those hopes were rapidly punctured, however, by the realisation that the hard things to teach a computer were not the achievements on which

humans pride themselves – logic, mathematics, chess, and so on – but common sense things which they take for granted. Computers cannot reliably navigate across a room, understand a children's story, or take a telephone message.

The problem is that logic, mathematics, chess and the like have well-defined formal rules which, given a good deal of labour, can be expressed in terms a computer can understand; day-to-day life does not. Philosophical arguments over whether or not computers ever will equal human performance centre on the SYMBOL PROCESSING HYPOTHESIS.

Today, active areas of AI research include:

- knowledge representation – that is the task of putting facts and knowledge into a machine;
- PLANNING;
- MACHINE LEARNING;
- DISTRIBUTED AI;
- reasoning – or teaching computers to use knowledge to create new knowledge, for example, by DEDUCTION.

More practically, 40 years of AI research have created many technologies sufficiently robust and useful to go to work in business, including:

- EXPERT SYSTEMS;
- NEURAL NETS;
- VISION;
- LANGUAGE UNDERSTANDING.

A brilliant chess move while the room is filling with smoke because the house is burning down does not show intelligence. If the capacity for brilliant chess moves without regard to life circumstances deserves a name, I would naturally call it "artificial intelligence".
Anatol Holt

ARTIFICIAL LIFE
The quest to make machines which can act as intelligently as insects. Instead of trying to under-

stand the world, as people do, artificial-life (A-life) researchers reckon it is better to try to build machines that can simply react to it, without conscious reflection, as ants and slugs presumably do. Rodney Brooks of the Massachusetts Institute of Technology, a leader in the field, argues that a more practical alternative to a robotic butler, say, might be a horde of "ant-bots" which scurry across the floor at night picking up dust in the same way that real ants pick up crumbs. While such creations are a long way off – if they are ever to arrive at all – studies in A-life have deepened understanding of how simple components can in combination give rise to great (and possibly useful) complexity. More practically, genetic algorithms enable computer programs to mimic biological evolution in adapting to their environment.

ASCII

Pronounced *as-key*, the American Standard Code for Information Interchange, a STANDARD for encoding the characters of the Roman alphabet (that is, a, b, c, and so on) as numbers which can be stored and manipulated by a computer. Alternative character-encoding schemes include EBCDIC.

ASSEMBLER

Or assembly language, the native language of computers. The nouns and verbs of assembler correspond directly to the functions of a specific MICROPROCESSOR chip: for example, adding two numbers, or extracting a number from MEMORY. In the 1960s and early 1970s most SOFTWARE was written in assembler. But the painstaking detail required caused delays and errors. Today programs are more easily written in higher-level languages – like ADA, C and COBOL – which are automatically translated back into their assembler equivalents (by a COMPILER) for execution on the computer.

ASYNCHRONOUS

Not having the same time clock. Most communications technologies assume that the clocks of sender and receiver can tick at different rates. This means that they have to include ways of communicating where each part of the signal starts and stops, to avoid, for example, the receiver taking the last half of the code for the letter a and the first half of the code of the letter z to come up with the letter o. But for most purposes it is easier to send start and stop signals than to keep the two clocks precisely synchronised. (Contrast to SYN-CHRONOUS.)

ASYNCHRONOUS DIGITAL SUBSCRIBER LOOP
See ADSL.

ASYNCHRONOUS TRANSFER MODE
The fastest of a new breed of telecoms switches. Like other PACKET switching devices, asynchronous transfer mode (ATM) routes DIGITAL DATA divided into small chunks, each a few BYTES long, called packets. Key to their speed is that ATM packets are all of a uniform size – 53 bytes – of which 48 are data. The remaining five carry INFORMATION about that data, notably its destination (to distinguish the many different transmissions that might be sharing a communications channel) and its priority (to distinguish, say, a videoconference, whose packets must arrive quickly, from a piece of E-MAIL, which can be delayed for a few milliseconds if necessary). Using ATM technology, researchers hope to build switches that can transmit data at speeds of gigabits per second, an order of magnitude or two faster than today's networks. That would make it as quick to send information across a NETWORK as to move it around within a single computer. In a very real sense, ATM could make vast networks act as a single computer cum telephone cum television cum...

ATM
See ASYNCHRONOUS TRANSFER MODE. This is also the acronym for automated teller machine: the hole-in-the-wall which dispenses bank notes on the insertion of a plastic card.

AUTOMATION

Doing a task automatically, without human intervention, usually by entrusting the work to a machine. The point of automation is typically to dispense with human skills, because they are either relatively expensive, or untrustworthy, or both. Many applications of information technology differ slightly from traditional mechanisation in that they require people to be kept in the LOOP, but using somewhat different skills, and doing somewhat different work, than they had done before (see INFOMATION).

So without entirely realising what has happened, the physician in the past two centuries has gradually relinquished his unsatisfactory attachment to subjective evidence, what the patient says, only to substitute devotion to technological evidence, what the machine says.
Stanley Reiser

B-TREE

A method of structuring DATA so that it can be accessed quickly. It is most often used for files stored on DISK, but it can be used for any collection of data that can be put into some order.

BACK OFFICE

Where the hard graft of the white-collar work is done: the FRONT OFFICE sells, the back office delivers. A stockbroker's back office, for example, handles the paperwork of transferring share ownership; a chemicals company's back office schedules production and delivery. Accounting and payroll are always in the back office. The back office is where computers were first applied in business, and the term still describes systems geared towards production and motivated by efficiency.

BACK-UP

To save a copy of DATA stored on a DISK on to another medium, usually tape or OPTICAL DISK. Back-up is meant to provide a reserve copy of data lest something terrible should happen to the disk.

BACKWARD CHAINING

See EXPERT SYSTEM.

BANDWIDTH

Loosely used to refer to the amount of INFORMATION or DATA communicated: a high-bandwidth communication is – or at least it should be – more informative than a low-bandwidth one. Strictly, bandwidth refers to the difference between the highest FREQUENCY that a given communications channel can carry and the lowest. Channels in which this difference is large can carry more data than those in which it is small. Indeed, given a strict mathematical definition of information, Harold Nyquist, a theoretician from the USA's Bell Labs, proved in 1924 that the maximum number of BITS a channel could carry was equal to twice the bandwidth.

BASIC

Abbreviation for Beginner's All-purpose Symbolic Instruction Code, an easy-to-learn programming language popular on the PERSONAL COMPUTER. Now increasingly superseded by more powerful languages like C.

BAT

A suffix which denotes to MICROSOFT'S DOS OPERATING SYSTEM that the FILE bearing it contains a SCRIPT, that is, a set of commands that the operating system should execute in order to automate a simple task. The file called *autoexec.bat* is executed automatically when the computer is first started, and is thus used to initialise and to customise the system.

BATCH PROCESSING

Describes a computer system which works to a rigorous and uninterruptable schedule. Jobs, for example a payroll, are scheduled for the hour when the computer next has free processing time. Once started, the job runs to completion. Interactive computers, by contrast, try to reschedule work on an ad hoc basis to respond to urgent and unexpected demands. Historically most MAINFRAME computers have used batch processing, which is largely responsible for their reputation as being inconvenient and annoying.

BAUD

A measure of the speed of DIGITAL communications equipment which is closely related to the maximum number of BITS that can be sent in a second.

BAYESIAN ANALYSIS

A form of statistics which calculates the probability of some event given knowledge of some related INFORMATION. For example, conventional statistics enable the calculation of the (small) probability that a given person has measles at any given moment. Bayesian statistics calculate the (larger) probability that the person has measles, given the knowledge that he is covered in spots. Named after the 18th-century British mathematician, Thomas Bayes, this technique is widely used in automated diagnosis (for obvious reasons).

BETA

The final stage of SOFTWARE quality testing. Before general release, selected people are typically given beta copies of software to use as if it were finished in order to see what, if anything, breaks.

BINARY

Loosely used to describe anything without shades of grey; that is, which can be either black or white, true or false, on or off. Strictly, it refers to a number system based on the number two. Instead of powers of ten, as in the DECIMAL system, numbers are expressed in terms of powers of two. The only allowable digits are zero and one. Thus 27 in decimal ($2 \times 10^1 + 7 \times 10^0$) is 11011 in binary ($1 \times 2^4 + 1 \times 2^3 + 0 \times 2^2 + 1 \times 2^1 + 1 \times 2^0$). This number system is convenient for describing electronic circuits, which are either on (with current) or off (without).

BIND

To associate a value with a variable.

BINHEX

A program to convert BINARY files into ASCII ones that can be sent over the INTERNET, most commonly used on MACINTOSH computers.

BIT

Abbreviation of binary digit, thus zero or one (see BINARY).

BIT MAP

A grid of dots which contains the information needed to display a picture on a computer screen or PRINTER. Typically each dot corresponds to the colour of a particular point, or PIXEL, on the screen. Display the dots in the appropriate rows and columns and, lo and behold, a picture appears. (The colour of dots, in turn, is coded as BITS, hence the name.)

This correspondence between dots in the bit map and points on the screen makes bit maps extremely easy to use on any given screen. But it also makes them extremely hard to move from one screen to another, because different screens lay out rows and columns in different proportions. (See also VECTOR GRAPHICS, of which the converse is true.)

BOGOSITY
A measure of ridiculousness used in slang by computer HACKERS. Derived from bogus.

BOOLEAN ALGEBRA
Provides a theoretical understanding of how computers compute. In the 19th century the British mathematician, George Boole, studied in detail formal rules for calculating with the values true and false, which underlie formal LOGIC. His work remained relatively obscure until the 1960s, when someone noticed that the true and false of Boole's logic correspond to the on or off of an electrical switch, and that Boole's rules of calculation could be used to understand better how those switches could add, subtract and calculate.

BOOT STRAP
Or boot, refers to the initial stages of starting up a computer. Usually the OPERATING SYSTEM loads programs from DISK into MEMORY. So what loads the operating system? The boot strap code, of course, which runs when the power is first turned on.

BOZO FILTER
See KILL FILE.

BRIDGE
Equipment used to connect two local area networks. Bridges can connect networks using different communication protocols (for example, TCP/IP and APPLETALK), as well as different transmission mechanisms (for example, ETHERNET and TOKEN RING). A ROUTER, by contrast, is used to connect networks with the same PROTOCOL.

B

BRITTLE
Describes computer systems that break suddenly and completely. A common fault of many programs, particularly ARTIFICIAL INTELLIGENCE programs, is that they work either perfectly or not at all. This is usually a bad thing. (Contrast to GRACEFUL DEGRADATION.)

BROADBAND
Loosely used to describe signals of high BANDWIDTH. It is specifically used to describe the use of (high-bandwidth) COAXIAL CABLE to transmit radio, television or other ANALOGUE signals that would typically be sent over the airwaves. Also used as a generic term for high speed telecommunications circuits and services.

BROADCAST
Describes a signal sent indiscriminately to all receivers with range, such as television, in contrast to point-to-point communication (like a telephone), or person-to-person communication (like conversation). With computer networks researchers are developing new forms of communication, between broadcast and point-to-point, called MULTICAST.

BTW
Abbreviation of By The Way, commonly used on the INTERNET, as in "BTW, have you heard the joke about…?"

BUFFER
A section of computer MEMORY, typically one used for temporary storage. A communications buffer, for example, acts as a kind of marshalling area for DATA coming into, or going out of, a computer.

BUG
An error or problem with computer HARDWARE or SOFTWARE. It is named after a moth, discovered by a computing pioneer, Grace Hopper, which immolated itself in the circuitry of an early computer. The computer was repaired by replacing a

damaged vacuum tube. The moth is now preserved in the Computer Museum in Cambridge, Massachusetts.

To err is human, and to blame it on a computer is even more so.

BULLETIN BOARD
A computer system used for posting electronic messages. Messages are organised into files on the bulletin board's HARD DISK, usually by topic. People can dial up the bulletin board and read what has been said on a given topic and, if they like, add their own comments. Little more is required to run a bulletin board than a PERSONAL COMPUTER and MODEM. By the early 1990s the USA alone had over 50,000 public bulletin boards, ranging from big commercial operations (like Prodigy, backed by IBM) to systems set up by teenagers in their bedrooms to share information with their friends.

BUS
The central wiring that connects together the components of a computer.

BYTE
Eight BITS, the most commonly used measure of DATA-storage capacity. Large HARD-DISK drives, for example, store gigabytes (that is, billions of bytes) of INFORMATION. A nibble is half a byte, or four bits.

C

C

The most popular programming language for personal computers and workstations. Created in the 1970s at Bell Labs by Dennis Ritchie, C was originally distributed with the UNIX OPERATING SYSTEM. It owes its popularity to its ability to express the nitty-gritty details of a computer's inner workings (to help achieve efficiency) with a certain elegance and abstraction (to help achieve comprehensibility by mere flesh and blood).

C++

An OBJECT-ORIENTED successor to C created by Bjarne Stroustrop at Bell Labs in the 1980s. Its name is a programming pun. To add one to a variable (say n) in C, a programmer would write n++. Hence C++ (for the one after C). Who says programmers don't have a sense of fun?

CACHE

A small area of very fast MEMORY, typically on a MICROPROCESSOR, which is used to store (what the machine hopes will be) the next instructions used in the computation, and thus to eliminate delays by making them available more rapidly than if they had to be fetched from the main DRAM.

CAD

Short for computer aided design. SOFTWARE which helps draughtsmen and graphic artists. Computers can greatly simplify the task of keeping technical drawings in the proper scale and perspective. They can manage libraries of ready-drawn objects, and, like word processors, computer-aided design programs greatly simplify the task of making alterations.

CALL CENTRE

A centralised facility for handling customer enquiries over the telephone; and a far more interesting place than it sounds. The technology of call centres is at the cutting edge of the integration of computers and communications. When someone calls, their telephone number is snatched automatically from the line and looked up in a DATABASE. If someone calling from that number has done business with the company before, all details are on screen when the call is answered. Meanwhile, in the background, a marketing analysis program compares that customer's purchases with those of its fellows to see what this customer might want to buy next, and then to prompt the salesperson into suggesting it.

This integration between computers and communications inspires many CIOS to see in them the future of office AUTOMATION. Not all of those who work with the technology will see this as a blessing. The automation can empower workers by putting INFORMATION at their finger-tips, but it can also turn them into script-following drones. All it takes is a slight push of management emphasis either way.

CALS
Short for Computer Aided Logistics and Support, an ambitious program led by the USA's Defense Department to set the standards necessary to automate military procurement. In theory, the standards cover all stages of production: bidding, design, manufacturing and documentation.

CAM
Short for Computer Aided Manufacturing, a generic term used to refer to shop-floor AUTOMATION.

CARRIER
The carrier is a constant signal into which information is encoded, typically by varying the carrier's FREQUENCY, AMPLITUDE, or both.

CASE
For computer aided software engineering, it is SOFTWARE which helps programmers. There are a variety of computer-aided software engineering tools. Some help keep track of different versions of an evolving program. Others help to find bugs. Yet others make it easy to design and build forms

on screen for entering and displaying DATA. A FOURTH-GENERATION LANGUAGE simplifies the task of writing programs that use a DATABASE.

> *Adding manpower to a late software project makes it later.*
> Fred Brooks, 1975

CASE-BASED REASONING
Techniques in ARTIFICIAL INTELLIGENCE, originally devised by Janet Kolodner of the Georgia Institute of Technology, which reason from precedent. In effect, the technology builds an electronic DATABASE which describes previous situations encountered and records the action taken then. When a new situation is met, the computer tries to find a past situation sufficiently similar that the same action will work again. The difficulty, of course, is defining similar. But Compaq, among others, has successfully used the technology to build up corporate databases which help new-comers share the knowledge of their more experienced colleagues.

CCITT
The French acronym for the International Consultative Committee for Telegraphy and Telephony, a group set up by United Nations treaty to set technical standards for the world's communication systems. Most countries are represented by their PTT. CCITT is most well-known in the computer world for the V STANDARDS and other standards used in DATA communications.

CDMA
Short for Code Division Multiple Access, a way of multiplexing a variety of signals on to a single communications channel. CDMA first makes several copies of each BIT to be transmitted. Then it combines each expanded group of bits with a special code, of the same length, and transmits the result. Many other transmitters may be sending their own (expanded and coded) signals on the same chan-

nel. So, at the other end, the receiver picks up all transmissions, effectively added together. But using the special code it can pick the signal it wants to listen to out of the jumble.

CDMA uses BANDWIDTH more flexibly than its chief technical rival TCMA, but there is less experience in using it. Both Europe and the USA are now trying to choose between the two for the next generation of wireless telephones and DATA networks.

CD-ROM
Short for Compact Disk, Read-Only Memory, the medium of choice for the first generation of MULTIMEDIA publishers. Compact disks, the same kind as are used for sound recording, can store a lot of DATA – about 640 megabytes, 600 or so times more than a FLOPPY DISK. That is enough to store the text from several hundred books, two hours of high-quality sound, an hour of television-quality video, or some combination of the above.

CELLULAR AUTOMATA
A mathematical creation useful for simulating complex, dynamic phenomena. Cellular automata are based on a grid of cells. Each cell contains a value. At each step of a computation, each cell calculates a new value based on the values of neighbouring cells. (For example, 1 if the sum of the values of surrounding cells is less than 4; otherwise 0.) Even simple rules can spawn immensely complex behaviour. With highly parallel computers to help with the computation, researchers are using cellular automata to improve their understanding of phenomena ranging from the flow of fluids to foetal development, all areas in which (presumably) simple local interactions create global behaviour of great complexity.

CELLULAR TELEPHONE
A wireless mobile telephone. The name refers to the overlapping NETWORK of radio receivers required to provide service to a mobile telephone. Each receiver's reception area is called a cell. For

technologists, the tricky part of building mobile telephone networks lies in ensuring a seamless hand-off for moving users (say in a car) as they move from one cell to another. For business planners, the trick is ensuring a sufficient capacity for a whole country (or indeed region) full of constantly moving subscribers.

CENTRAL PROCESSING UNIT
See CPU.

CGI
Short for Common Gateway Interface, a PROTOCOL used to enable programs to work together over the WORLD WIDE WEB. With the CGI, for example, clicking on a HYPERTEXT link to a person's name might call up an E-MAIL program to send e-mail to them.

CHECKSUM
A way of detecting errors in computer DATA. The BINARY values of the data are added together to form a checksum. The checksum is transmitted with the data. If the sum of the binary values of the received data differs from the received checksum, then something has gone wrong.

CIM
Short for Computer Integrated Manufacturing, which describes efforts to link CAD to electronically controlled machine tools to enable designers simply to push a button and, whoosh, designs are automatically translated into machining instructions, and thus into real parts.

CIO
Short for Chief Information Officer, a job which brings together responsibility for corporate INFORMATION and knowledge with responsibility for managing the technology which stores and communicates it. In theory, CIOS are perfectly positioned to lead corporate change; in practice, their jobs are also highly insecure.

C

CIRCUIT SWITCHED
How a telephone works. When a connection is made, sender and receiver have the BANDWIDTH of the intervening line all to themselves for the duration of the connection, whether they use it or not. (Contrast to PACKET SWITCHED.)

CISC
Short for Complex Instruction Set Computing, an approach to the design of microprocessors, popular in the 1970s, which tried to pack as many functions as possible into the instruction set, or set of commands which that MICROPROCESSOR could understand. Unfortunately the complexity of creating all these instructions slows chips down. So CISC has been superseded by RISC, a minimalist approach to chip design.

CLIENT SERVER
Describes computer systems which divide labour among machines linked by networks. Rather like Adam Smith's pin factory, each machine does what it is suited for. So a FILE SERVER is equipped with lots of DISK space to store DATA; a name server holds the information necessary to serve as the NETWORK's telephone directory. Not only does specialisation avoid duplication of effort, but it also makes client-server systems easier to improve. If, say, all heavy-duty number-crunching is done by a calculation server, then simply replacing that one machine with a more powerful one can improve the performance of the whole network.

CLIPPER
A controversial encryption STANDARD proposed by the US government. Anyone wishing to encrypt sensitive information with Clipper technology would have to give the government a copy of the key with which to decode it. The government says this is crucial for national security; many others, including a significant chunk of the computer industry, view it as an outrageous invasion of privacy.

CMOS

Short for Complementary Metal Oxide Semiconductor, a way of making a SEMICONDUCTOR with relatively low power consumption. CMOS chips are often used in laptop computers and other battery-powered devices.

COAXIAL CABLE

The thick wire through which cable television and other high-BANDWIDTH signals travel (also called coax). The thickness comes from an extra layer of metal mesh wrapped around the copper-wire core, to guard against electrical interference.

COBOL

Abbreviation for Common Business Oriented Language, a computer language designed for business use in the 1960s and now the world's most widely used programming language. Its verbose structure, created to read like English, creates a kind of mandatory mediocrity, making it as hard to write really bad programs as it is to write really good ones.

COMMAND-LINE INTERFACE

Describes a computer which provides a prompt, or command-line, for the user to type in commands. This is in contrast to a MENU-DRIVEN INTERFACE, which asks the user to choose from a menu of commands displayed on the screen. Command-line interfaces, like that offered by Microsoft's DOS, offer users great flexibility, but they require them to remember the exact magical incantations which will induce the computer to act. Menu-driven interfaces, like the MACINTOSH, are easy to use – particularly for those not terribly familiar with the system – but harder to customise or to do complicated things with.

COMMON CARRIER

A communications company which carries information for all. It also refers to regulatory regimes designed to ensure non-discriminatory access to communications networks.

COMPILER

A piece of SOFTWARE which translates programs written in high-level languages like C and COBOL into the MACHINE CODE which computers can act upon. Using a compiler, creating and running a program requires two separate steps. First the compiler translates the source code into a separate FILE of machine code, often optimising as it does so to make the program run as fast as possible. Then the computer runs the programs by executing the instructions in this separate machine code file. This is in contrast to an INTERPRETER, which does the job in a single step, translating and executing the source code itself. Interpreted programs run more slowly than compiled ones, but they are quicker and easier to DEBUG.

COMPOSITE MONITOR

A colour MONITOR that mixes together red, green and blue signals for ease of input, and thereby suffers somewhat inferior resolution compared with an RGB MONITOR.

COMPRESSION

Techniques for reducing the amount of DATA needed to convey some amount of INFORMATION. (See, for example, RUN-LENGTH ENCODING, LZW ALGORITHM, HUFFMAN CODING.)

COMPUTER AIDED DESIGN

See CAD.

COMPUTER AIDED LOGISTICS AND SUPPORT

See CALS.

COMPUTER AIDED MANUFACTURING

See CAM.

COMPUTER AIDED SOFTWARE ENGINEERING

See CASE.

COMPUTER INTEGRATED MANUFACTURING

See CIM.

COMPUTER SUPPORTED CO-OPERATIVE WORK

The use of computers to help people work together more productively. Computer supported co-operative work (CSCW) divides into two broad categories. GROUPWARE is typically used to share INFORMATION among a group. WORKFLOW prompts users through a complex task, reminding them at each step of the way what should be done next.

Although the distinction is not always clear-cut, groupware, like decision-support systems, exists largely to help people make up their own minds. The assumption is that, given the right information, they are knowledgeable enough to make the right decision. Workflow systems, by contrast, assume that the machine knows best.

CONNECTION-ORIENTED

The same as CIRCUIT SWITCHED.

If the Internet's present 100% a year rate of growth continues, everyone on the planet will be connected by 2003.

CONNECTIONIST

Describes computing done with a NEURAL NET. In general, connectionists argue that – in silicon as in the human brain – it is complex connections and feedback between individual computing units (or neurons) that give a machine the power to tackle complex problems, not the raw capabilities of any one.

COPYLEFT

An alternative to copyright created by Richard Stallman. Programs distributed under copyleft must be made available without charge, with full source code.

CORBA

Short for Common Object Request Broker Architecture, a would-be STANDARD to enable OBJECT-ORIENTED programs to co-operate over networks.

To print a document on a LASER PRINTER today, a person has to find the available printers and pick one. CORBA would enable a document automatically to send out a query across the NETWORK to find the available printer which best suited its needs. (See also OLE and OPENDOC.)

CORE
An antiquated term used to refer to computer MEMORY.

CPU
Short for central processing unit. The brains of a computer; the chip or chips that execute programs.

CRACKER
A malicious HACKER; someone whose joy in life is breaking into other people's computer and communication systems and then trashing them.

CRASH
A verb or noun describing what happens when a computer ceases to function. It originally derived from DISK crash, which described what happens when the magnetic heads designed to read information from a disk drive instead bury themselves into it. Synonyms for crash include wedged, down, hosed, sucking mud, hung, catatonic, in Helen Keller mode and others too descriptive to print.

CRC
See CYCLIC REDUNDANCY CHECK.

CSCW
See COMPUTER SUPPORTED CO-OPERATIVE WORK.

CURSOR
An ICON, often an arrow, which marks on the screen the focus of attention of a computer program. Text typed at the keyboard will be inserted at the location of the cursor in the text. Clicking the MOUSE will select the item pointed to by the cursor.

C

CYBERNETICS
The science of control systems, from thermostats to auto-pilots. Developed by Norbert Wiener at the Massachusetts Institute of Technology in the 1940s, one of the central themes of cybernetics is the notion of feedback, the idea that a system's past can affect its future. Negative feedback is what a thermostat does: the more heat there was in the past, the less there will be in future. Population growth is governed by positive feedback: the more bunnies there are today, the more the population will grow tomorrow.

CYBERSPACE
The virtual geography created by computers and networks; the world behind the screen. Perhaps the most vivid vision of cyberspace comes from William Gibson. In his science-fiction novel *Neuromancer* – which for many is the defining vision of the techno-future – he describes, quoting from an imaginary children's show being transmitted across the NETWORK of the future, a virtual world in which DATA is made visible, and the network becomes geography:

> *Cyberspace. A consensual hallucination experienced daily by billions of legitimate operators, in every nation, by children being taught mathematical concepts…. A graphic representation of data extracted from the banks of every computer in the human system. Unthinkable complexity. Lines of light ranged in the nonspace of the mind, clusters and constellations of data. Like city lights, receding…*

CYCLIC REDUNDANCY CHECK
A brain-bogglingly complicated calculation which is used to detect errors in DATA being sent over communications lines.

D

DAEMON

A program which sits unobtrusively in the background waiting for some event to happen, which it then deals with. In the UNIX OPERATING SYSTEM, for example, daemons handle the delivery of E-MAIL and other NETWORK requests.

DATA

Raw facts, which are not necessarily relevant to anything anybody wants to know; in contrast to INFORMATION, which is data that answers a question.

DATA DICTIONARY

A list of all the different sorts of DATA contained in a computing system, including details of standard formats, how they are stored on the computer and what they represent.

DATA-LINK LAYER

That part of the SEVEN LAYER REFERENCE MODEL which concerns technologies for error correction and access to the underlying communications medium. Technologies working at the data-link level try to create the illusion of a perfect, error-free transmission line for the packets that come and go across it. Different approaches use a variety of different methods to detect and correct errors.

DATA MINING

Techniques for sifting through huge quantities of DATA, typically using powerful computers, to try to find INFORMATION, typically in the form of either statistical correlations or rare facts.

DATA MODEL

A formal description of the sorts of DATA a computer system should keep on any given subject. For example, the data model for a customer might include name, address and age. Although they sound simple, data models are rapidly becoming highly complex because different people want to know different things. To be assigned to the team building a corporate data model is to be given a Sisyphean task, unlikely to be finished before your career has run its course.

DATA PROCESSING

The really boring work done by computers, including payroll, accountancy, and so on. It includes most programs written in COBOL.

DATA PROTECTION

Refers to regulation concerning the privacy of DATA, typically personal data. Most countries require companies which hold INFORMATION about their customers to divulge what information they have and how they got it. Many further require companies to register their information holdings with a data protection board, which is charged with looking after citizens' interests. None of these solutions really work, though. All seem to be bureaucratic, ineffective, or both. So data protection and privacy will for years continue to be one of the most heated issues in the regulation of CYBERSPACE.

DATABASE

A computerised filing system which forms the core of most corporate computer systems. Databases store and retrieve INFORMATION, and as the number of different kinds of information kept on computers increases, databases are evolving to cope.

The most common database now in use is the RELATIONAL DATABASE. A few banks still use a HIERARCHICAL DATABASE, but most are struggling to convert to the newer relational technology. For the future, developers are working on the OBJECT DATABASE, which makes it easier to store video, graphics and other complex data alongside the sorts of text and data that most databases now contain.

Each database also has a query language, which allows its users to access its data. The most popular one nowadays is STRUCTURED QUERY LANGUAGE.

DBMS
Short for Database Management System (see DATABASE).

DEBUG
To correct errors in a computer program (see BUG).

DEC
See DIGITAL EQUIPMENT CORPORATION.

DECIMAL
Describes the number system based on counting by tens which most people use every day. (Contrast to BINARY and HEXADECIMAL, the number systems which most computers use every day.)

DECISION-SUPPORT SYSTEM
A computer system designed to provide the INFORMATION needed to help people make up their minds, as distinct from an EXPERT SYSTEM, which is a computer system designed to make up people's minds for them. The advantage the computer can bring to decision support is that it can provide information either more quickly than would otherwise be possible, or in greater detail, or both.

DECLARATIVE PROGRAMMING
A style of programming that allows the programmer to concentrate on what is to be done, without worrying too much about how. PROLOG is a good example of declarative programming. It allows programs to be written as a DATABASE of facts, supplemented by statements about those facts. The program computes by trying to make those statements true, and in theory the programmer does not have to worry too much about how it does so. By contrast procedural programming languages like C and LISP require the programmer to state exactly the procedures the program is to follow, step by detailed step.

DEDUCTION
Reasoning which proceeds from premises to con-

D

clusions. Typically deduction involves both facts
and rules of reasoning. Given, for a simple example, the rule "all men are mortal" and the fact
"Fred is a man", then we can deduce "Fred is mortal". (See also ABDUCTION and INDUCTION.)

DEMON
See DAEMON.

DESKTOP PUBLISHING
Describes HARDWARE and SOFTWARE for personal
computers that can lay out text and graphics at a
fraction of the cost of a large publishing house,
but with quality nearly as high.

DIGITAL
DATA stored as a sequence of discrete BINARY digits,
as opposed to analogue, which is data stored as a
continuously varying signal. (See ANALOGUE for a
discussion of the pros and cons of each.)

---

*There is no reason for any individual to have a
computer in their home.*
Ken Olsen, 1977

DIGITAL EQUIPMENT CORPORATION
Creator of the MINICOMPUTER. Minicomputers typically cost hundreds of thousands of dollars rather
than the millions required for a MAINFRAME, and
were thus suitable for smaller companies.
Founded by Ken Olsen in a former textile mill in
Maynard, Massachusetts, Digital Equipment Corporation (DEC)'s first series of computers was pre-
fixed with the initials PDP; its second was called
the VAX. DEC failed to adapt quickly to the challenge of smaller, cheaper microcomputers, however. By the early 1990s it had tumbled from its
position as one of the computer industry's most-
admired companies and its founder and former
chairman, Mr Olsen, had been ousted by his
board.

DIGITAL SIGNATURE

A cryptographic technique which ensures that an electronic document really does come from the person whose name is at the top. It usually relies on PUBLIC-KEY CRYPTOGRAPHY.

DISK

A medium for the storage of DATA. Most disks now in use are magnetically coated, and store the 1s and 0s of DIGITAL data by imprinting (or not imprinting) a tiny magnetic field on the disk. Optical disks work on a similar basis with a laser and a reflective (or non-reflective) coating. (See also OPTICAL DISK, FLOPPY DISK and HARD DISK.)

DISTRIBUTED AI

An approach to ARTIFICIAL INTELLIGENCE (AI) based on the hope that many small intelligences can do more than one big one. Traditional AI would, for example, try to improve the flow of road traffic by creating a single supreme intelligence, which knew everything that went on the roads and tried to optimise globally. The snag is that many problems become unworkably large and complex if tackled all at once. So distributed AI tries to solve big problems as a series of small ones, each tackled by a different problem-solving agent.

Given this approach, distributed AI inevitably shifts the emphasis of research. Instead of trying to eke the most out of each problem-solver, the distributed approach tries also to find ways in which problem-solver agents can co-ordinate their efforts via negotiation, co-operation and delegation.

DISTRIBUTED COMPUTING

The practice of using different computers, linked across a NETWORK, to solve computing problems co-operatively. (Contrast to MAINFRAME and see also CLIENT SERVER.)

DOMAIN

A named part of a NETWORK. It is most often used to refer to one of the independent networks

D

which make up the INTERNET. Under Internet addressing conventions, any computer with an address ending in, say, *dog.com* is said to be in the *dog* domain. This means that it shares the same administrator with other computers in the same domain. Given the global scope of computer networks, sharing the same domain obviously has nothing to do with physical proximity.

DOS

Short for Disk Operating System, MICROSOFT'S OPERATING SYSTEM for desktop computers. Originally incarnated as QDOS, for quick-and-dirty operating system, DOS was written by Tim Patterson at Seattle Computer Products. Bill Gates bought the rights to the program for $250,000 when he discovered that IBM, which had approached him to license his implementation of the BASIC programming language, might also be interested in an operating system. The rest is history.

DOT MATRIX PRINTER

See MATRIX PRINTER.

DOUBLE-PRECISION ARITHMETIC

FLOATING-POINT ARITHMETIC, performed with a relatively large number of bytes in order to try to preserve accuracy, despite the inevitable ROUNDING ERRORS which stem from trying to fit numbers with potentially unlimited digits beyond the decimal point into a limited number of bytes in the computer.

DOWNLOAD

To transfer DATA from a remote (usually large) computer to a local (usually small) one. (Contrast to UPLOAD.)

DRAM

Short for Dynamic Random Access Memory, the MEMORY chips used by most computers. DRAM stores BITS as tiny electric charges on a grid of tiny circuits. Each bit's charge (or lack of charge) can be accessed independently, by specifying the row

D

and column of the circuit on which the charge is held, hence random access. But to keep costs down, charge is held in such a way that it gradually dwindles if left on its own and thus must be constantly refreshed (hence dynamic). This refreshing cycle makes DRAM slightly slower than SRAM (static RAM), but the extra nanoseconds are considered well worth the cost saving.

Today DRAM is usually sold mounted on SIMMS for convenience of use. The largest size now widely available contains 16 megabits on each chip, but 64 megabit chips are coming out of the research labs.

In 1980 a megabyte of DRAM cost about $2,500; by 1995 the price had fallen to about $25.

DUMP
To record verbatim, without any attempt to order, usually for archival purposes; roughly the computer's equivalent of stream of consciousness.

DUPLEX
A communication channel which allows messages to travel in both directions at once. (Contrast to SIMPLEX.)

E-MAIL

Short for electronic mail. Just as the name implies, a message sent electronically from one computer to another. E-mail is typically text, but emerging standards for MULTIMEDIA mail, notably MIME, enable anything that can be put in DIGITAL form to be e-mailed. Roughly a fifth of the traffic on the INTERNET consists of e-mail.

President Clinton's e-mail address is:
president@whitehouse.gov
Bill Gates's e-mail address is: billg@microsoft.com

EBCDIC

Abbreviation for Enhanced Binary Coded Decimal Interchange Code, a STANDARD for coding text characters as numbers used on IBM mainframes. Almost as complicated to use as it is to say, EBCDIC is being superseded by ASCII and other more modern character codes.

EDI

Short for Electronic Data Interchange, the automatic, electronic exchange of corporate DATA, particularly boring, nitty-gritty stuff like parts orders, manufacturing instructions or inventory data.

EISA

Abbreviation for Extended Industry Standard Architecture, a standard BUS to carry DATA between the MICROPROCESSOR of an IBM-COMPATIBLE PERSONAL COMPUTER and MEMORY, disks and other peripherals. EISA will accept HARDWARE add-ons created for the ISA bus of the original IBM PC, but, given more capable equipment, it can also carry more data faster than the original.

ELECTRONIC FRONTIER

A phrase coined by a writer and activist, John Perry Barlow, to describe the challenge of creating laws and customs to govern CYBERSPACE. Together with a SOFTWARE entrepreneur, Mitch Kapor, Mr Barlow founded the Electronic Frontier Foundation to lobby for electronic civil rights. Mr Barlow was then living in Pinedale, Wyoming. He has since moved to New York City.

ELECTRONIC MAIL
See E-MAIL.

ELIZA
A program created by Joseph Weizenbaum to mimic a Rogerian psychoanalyst. Using simple pattern-matching techniques, Eliza responded to statements with questions; for example, the statement "I'm unhappy" might generate "Why are you unhappy?". Much to Mr Weizenbaum's surprise people attributed great intelligence to Eliza and became deeply emotionally involved in conversations with it. Today the Eliza effect refers to the human inclination to attribute unwarranted intelligence to computer systems, and their bitter disappointment when the computers fail to live up to their unjustified expectations.

EMACS
Short for Editing Macros. Created by Richard Stallman, a legendary HACKER, EMACS is probably the most popular WORD PROCESSOR for the UNIX OPERATING SYSTEM.

EMERGENT PROPERTY
An interesting and useful side-effect of a complex system. It is possible – perhaps common – for a system to achieve collectively goals which none of its components aim at individually. Economists, for example, have shown that, under many conditions, market competition provides a globally optimal distribution of resources, even though all the market participants are trying simply to get as much for themselves as they can.

ENTITY-RELATIONSHIP MODEL
An approach commonly used in SYSTEMS ANALYSIS which, as the name suggests, maps out the sorts of things a computer system might have to represent and the relationships between them. An entity-

relationship model for a library card catalogue, for example, might describe an entity called a book. The entry for book might further be linked to a person's name, with a relationship of author.

EOF
Short for End Of File. The name says it all really.

EPROM
Abbreviation for Erasable, Programmable, Read-Only Memory, a chip that can store DATA indefinitely (like any other ROM) but that can be erased and reprogrammed; unlike some forms of ROM which, once programmed, are fixed forever.

ESCAPE CHARACTER
A special character to denote that the character to follow has a special meaning. For example, an escape character followed by the letter c on some computer systems interrupts a program; while c alone is just c.

ETHERNET
A form of LOCAL AREA NETWORK, originally invented by Robert Metcalfe of Rank Xerox's Palo Alto Research Laboratory. It differs from a TOKEN-RING NETWORK chiefly in the way in which it mediates access to the network. In a token-ring network, computers constantly pass around an electronic token, and they can send DATA only if they hold the token. In Ethernet, by contrast, computers can send data any time they do not hear another computer already sending. If two send simultaneously, the collision is detected (because the data is garbled), and the two each wait a random period of time before trying again. In most circumstances Ethernet's *laissez-faire* approach is more efficient than token-ring's rigid discipline, except when network traffic is very heavy. Ethernet has a maximum capacity of about 10m BITS per second.

ETHERTALK
A fast version of APPLE's proprietary APPLETALK technology for local area networks, which, as the

E

name suggests, works on ETHERNET.

EUDORA
Named after the author, Eudora Welty, Eudora is a popular program for sending and receiving E-MAIL.

EXE
A suffix which denotes executable files (that is, programs) in the DOS OPERATING SYSTEM.

EXECUTIVE INFORMATION SYSTEM
A DECISION-SUPPORT SYSTEM for executives.

EXPERT SYSTEM
A computer system that tries to capture the knowledge of a human expert. Typically, the knowledge is stored as a series of if-then rules: for example, an expert system to diagnose computer faults might include the rules, "if the computer is unplugged, it has no power" and "if the machine has no power, then the screen is dark".

Large expert systems – with more than a hundred or so rules – rapidly become unwieldy. But miniature decision-makers can serve a variety of useful roles. They are used to help keep blast furnaces running smoothly in steel mills, to enable photocopiers to diagnose their own faults and dial a repairman, to suggest attractive formats for word-processed documents and to advise welfare applicants on which benefits they may be eligible for.

In the mid-1980s, when expert systems burst into the commercial world, many claimed that the systems would soon replace many skilled workers. They haven't – and won't. The biggest reason why expert systems will stay in the background is simply the narrowness of their knowledge. Like *idiots savants*, the machines are totally incompetent outside of their narrow realm of expertise. They can advise on the minutiae of, say, sickness benefit. But they haven't a clue what it is to be sick. So expert systems are most useful when working closely with a real person. The machine can help the person to remember details; the person can bring the machine's expertise to bear on the real world.

FACSIMILE
See FAX.

FAQ
Short for Frequently Asked Questions. For many of the topics under discussion on the INTERNET, particularly on a USENET NEWS GROUP, it is customary to maintain a beginner's guide, answering the most frequently asked questions on the topic. (For example, the FAQ for the news group *alt.sex* answers questions like: "What are some good positions to try out?" and "Can I be replaced by a vibrator?") Newcomers with NETIQUETTE read the FAQ before asking a question that may have been asked and answered a thousand times before; others get a FLAME.

FAX
From facsimile. A machine that transmits the image of a document electronically.

FDDI
Short for Fibre Distributed Data Interface, a high-BANDWIDTH LOCAL AREA NETWORK which uses FIBRE-OPTIC cable to transmit DATA at up to 100m BITS per second, ten times the speed of ETHERNET.

FIBRE OPTIC
A fine glass fibre which transmits light, much the same as a copper wire transmits electricity. Because it can be switched on or off extremely rapidly – much faster than an electric current – fibre optic can carry far more DATA than conventional copper wire.

FIDONET
A global computer NETWORK created for and by users of personal computers. Like USENET, FidoNet was a store-and-forward network; messages hopped from machine to machine, each sending the message a step nearer its destination. FidoNet has now largely been absorbed by the more technically sophisticated INTERNET.

FIELD

A component of an entry in a DATABASE. The IN-FORMATION in a database is composed of records, which in turn are composed of fields. Each RECORD corresponds to an individual entry, such as information about a particular customer. That record will be made up of a collection of fields, each containing a particular piece of DATA. For a customer record, for example, fields might well include name, date of birth, sex, and so on.

FIFO

First In, First Out, a method of managing incoming and outgoing DATA. FIFO dictates that the first piece of data to arrive will also be the first to be used. Although data may be stored temporarily in a BUFFER should more come in than can be immediately processed, FIFO guarantees that data will be processed in the order in which it arrives, in contrast to LIFO, which usually changes the order. Accounting has procedures for managing inventory with the same names, which work in exactly the same way.

FILE

The organising unit of a computer DISK. Computer files are by intention roughly analogous to the sort found in a filing cabinet: a collection of (presumably logically related) information stored together under a single name.

FILE SERVER

A machine on a NETWORK whose job it is to store files of DATA for other, linked computers. Typically the file server has more DISK space, and faster technology for accessing it, than other machines. Storing files centrally avoids duplication and makes administration easier.

FINGER

The name of a program used to get information about a computer user over a NETWORK. On the INTERNET, for example, typing *finger bloggs@somewhere.com* will usually produce a list of the full names and E-MAIL addresses of everyone named *bloggs* on the *somewhere.com* network.

FIREWALL

HARDWARE, but more usually SOFTWARE, designed to protect networked systems from damage by outsiders, while maintaining connectivity. The firewall sits between a local NETWORK and the big, wide world (usually the INTERNET). To protect the local network from evil-intentioned intruders, the firewall may admit only designated users, or allow only designated commands to be issued from outside. Balancing flexibility with SECURITY is, needless to say, a perennial headache in designing firewalls.

FIRST IN, FIRST OUT

See FIFO.

FLAME

A rude and abusive electronic communication. Electronic communication seems to lend itself to extreme forthrightness, perhaps because typing at a screen provides much of the emotion-raising interactivity of a conversation, but none of the interactive cues that signal when the person you are typing to is about to punch you in the face, or cry. Outbursts of mutual forthrightness on networks are called flame wars, and are generally discouraged.

FLAT FILE

A DATA FILE with only minimal structure. To speed access, many DATABASE technologies carefully structure the data in files so that the particular INFORMATION can be located on the DISK as quickly as possible (see, for example, B-TREE). Flat files have no such structure, and are thus typically quicker and cheaper to write information to, but slower to read from.

FLOATING-POINT ARITHMETIC

Arithmetic done with what mathematicians call REAL NUMBERS, that is, numbers with a decimal point in them. (Contrast to INTEGER arithmetic.)

A perennial problem with floating-point arithmetic is loss of precision. Some real numbers theoretically require an infinite number of digits to the right of the decimal point; 1 divided by 3, for example. Many more require more such digits than can fit into the slice of computer MEMORY allocated to store a representation of the number. Over time these ROUNDING ERRORS compound each other, making computer calculations wildly inaccurate if steps are not taken to overcome the problem.

FLOPPY DISK

A portable form of computer DISK, used to record relatively small quantities of electronic DATA. Floppy disks originally consisted of a round piece of cardboard, coated with a magnetic recording material similar to that used in recording tape. They were soft and floppy, hence the name. More modern, higher-capacity floppy disks are made of magnetically coated plastic, and they are in fact quite stiff. But somehow the word stiffy has never caught on as a replacement for floppy.

FLOW CHART

A kind of blueprint for building a computer program. Flow charts represent graphically not only the actions taken by a program as it executes, but also the choices it makes.

FLOW CONTROL

Procedures to manage the flow of DATA across a computer channel, typically to ensure that the receiving computer is not flooded with more information that it can handle. One commonly used method of flow control is XON XOFF, which sends a special signal, XON, to start transmission and another, XOFF, to interrupt it.

FORTH

A programming language which views the world through computer-coloured glasses. Specifically, it requires that programs be written in terms of stacks, a way of organising the work of calculation that is convenient for computers. It comes quite naturally to some people but apparently not enough to make Forth a really popular language, like c.

FOURTH-GENERATION LANGUAGE
A programming language, often linked directly with a specific DATABASE, which tries to provide ready-made tools to do common tasks, like laying out a screen or printing a report. The hope, which is sometimes realised, is that programmers will become more productive if they can use ready-made tools instead of building their own. The problem, however, is that the ready-made tools often do not do what is required and so must be time-consumingly modified. At the same time, the computing resources required by fourth-generation languages can make programs large and slow; another failed panacea.

FORTRAN
Acronym derived from Formula Translation, an early programming language created at IBM and particularly suited for mathematical number-crunching, for which it is still used.

FRAME PROBLEM
One of the classic problems in ARTIFICIAL INTELLIGENCE (AI), the frame problem concerns limiting the consequences of actions. When we say, for example, "the boy hit the ball", we instinctively assume that, while the ball moves, objects not mentioned – the cap on the boy's head, for example, or the shoes on his feet – stay the same. Or at least the cap and the shoes do not move as far as the ball does. One of the nastier aspects of the frame problem is that deciding what changes matter to the description of the problem is often highly subjective. Worse still, instinctive assumptions involve deep issues about the "connectedness" of things which are hard to translate into a form that a computer can understand.

Today's solutions to the frame problem are

frame axioms which state explicitly what each action changes and what it does not. But these solutions in turn raise their own problems. First, they add bulk and complication to AI's descriptions of the world. Second, they are hard to get right. Predicting the consequences of actions can be tricky, and frame axioms can introduce errors and contradictions of their own.

FRAME RELAY

A PACKET switching PROTOCOL, typically used for a WIDE AREA NETWORK, which can transmit data at up to 2m bits per second. While much faster than most LEASED LINES, which provide tens or hundreds of thousands of bits per second, this is still much slower than a LOCAL AREA NETWORK, most of which carry about 10m bits per second.

FREQUENCY

The rate of oscillation of a communications signal. It is typically measured in HERTZ, or cycles per second.

FROBNICATE

HACKER slang for twiddling dials and fiddling with controls just to see what they do; often abbreviated to frob.

FRONT OFFICE

That part of the business that deals directly with the customer – making sales, marketing, and so on. Although computers began their career in the BACK OFFICE they are moving to the front office with the advent of order-entry systems, marketing information published on the WORLD WIDE WEB and sales people carrying laptops.

In terms of traffic generated, the three most important uses of the Internet are FTP, the World Wide Web and USENET news groups (for electronic conversation).

FTP

Short for File Transfer Protocol. This refers to both

the program which transfers files from one computer to another across the INTERNET, and the technical standards which it uses. Bulk transfers of DATA with FTP make up about a third of Internet traffic.

FUNCTIONAL PROGRAMMING

Programming languages, like LISP, which are based on a mathematical theory of functions. The hope is to do away – as far as possible – with the variables in which conventional programs store values. The snag with variables is that, if one part of the program sets, say, x equal to 5, there is no guarantee that another part of the program will not have set it to 7 by the time it is next used, with potentially unpredictable results. Functional programming tries to overcome this by not storing values but by calculating each one afresh with a new function (which is simply something that calculates and returns a value). A snag with this approach, however, is that calculating each value afresh can consume huge quantities of time and/or MEMORY.

FUZZY LOGIC

A formal method of DEDUCTION which substitutes various shades of maybe for the stark, true-or-false choice of classical LOGIC. Take, for example, fat. In predicate logic, people either are fat, or they are not; there is no middle ground. So if a computer is to reason about fatness, its programmer has to devise an arbitrary weight at which people go from being non-fat to being fat. Fuzzy logic, by contrast, enables a computer to reason in terms of degrees of fatness, more like people do.

Not surprisingly, it typically works with percentages. Instead of an arbitrary threshold value at which somebody becomes fat, each possible weight is assigned a percentage value which indicates just how fat it is. At one extreme, fashion models would be 0% fat; towards the other extreme, Santa Claus might be, say, 90% fat; while only people with severe medical problems are 100% fat. These percentages will inevitably be somewhat arbitrary. The real advantage of fuzzy logic is not its (in)ability to quantify the unquantifiable, but its ability to reason with it.

At the heart of fuzzy logic are rules for reasoning with the percentages that denote the fuzzy categorisation of objects. Various approaches have been proposed for the task of combining "sort of fat" with "sort of short" to determine whether or not a person could be considered "short and fat". The solutions turn out to be particularly valuable for creating control systems for small appliances, like washing machines, which have to figure out how to behave when confronted with a "pretty small" load of "quite dirty" clothes.

G

GATEWAY
A device that connects two different computer systems or networks, particularly those using different technical standards or communications protocols.

GEEK
Like a NERD, someone who has devoted time to technology at the expense of more normal life. Recently, as technical knowledge has become fashionable, a new breed has arisen: the chic geek.

There are no bad haircuts in cyberspace.
Dave Barry

GENETIC ALGORITHM
A rough equivalent of Darwinian selection – survival of the fittest – used to breed SOFTWARE that is suited for a particular task. There are two basic components of any genetic algorithm: some measure of fitness, or success at a given task, and some analogue of breeding, whereby old software creates new software that behaves somewhat like its parents and somewhat differently. The basic procedure is to test a collection of programs on the task at hand, measure their fitness, and then allow only the fittest to breed. Given that computers can breed several generations in the blink of an eye, evolution proceeds quickly inside the machine. Genetic algorithms have bred successful solutions to many problems, including picking investment opportunities and monitoring suspicious financial transactions.

GEOSTATIONARY
Describes a satellite whose orbit is so synchronised with the rotation of the earth that it effectively hovers over the same spot. This property is useful for communications satellites, because the ground stations always know where to point their transmissions, and, once found, the satellite never moves out of range. But the positions where geo-

---

stationary (GEO) satellites can be located are already growing crowded.

GIF

Short for Graphics Information File, a widely used STANDARD for the format of the DATA needed to store images in a computer FILE. (See also JPEG, TIFF and PICT.)

GIGA-

Strictly, the prefix denotes a billion. In the computer world, however, it refers to 1,073,741,824, the nearest power of two.

GIGO

Short for Garbage In, Garbage Out, a pithy way of saying that the quality of the answers a system can give depends on the quality of the information given it to reason with. Truer words …

Computers are useless. They can only give you answers.
Pablo Picasso

GLOBAL POSITIONING SYSTEM
See GPS.

GLOBAL SYSTEM FOR MOBILE
See GSM.

GNU

Short for Gnu's Not Unix, which is the sort of self-referential pun beloved of computer programmers accustomed to writing programs which can recursively call themselves to get work done. It is the brand name of a collection of programs created by Richard Stallman and his fellow hackers at MIT. They replace, and in some cases improve upon, the standard components of the UNIX OPERATING SYSTEM, including COMPILERS and NETWORK utilities. All are distributed under COPYLEFT.

G

GOPHER
A collection of programs that make it easier to find information on the INTERNET. While TELNET and FTP require knowledge of specific FILE names and computers, Gopher can find material by subject category. Gopher was named after the school mascot of the University of Minnesota, where it was developed. Although still widely used, it has been overshadowed by the growth of the WORLD WIDE WEB.

GPS
Short for Global Positioning System, a satellite-based system which can determine the location of someone on the ground to within a few hundred metres. Originally developed for the military, GPS is rapidly finding civilian use, particularly as the necessary transceivers are shrinking to palm size. Someday your palm-top computer may be able not only to recommend the nearest good Chinese restaurant in a strange city, but also to guide you to it.

GRACEFUL DEGRADATION
Describes resilient machines or systems that do not break all at once, but keep soldiering on even if some components are broken. (Contrast to BRITTLE.)

GRAMMAR
A formal specification of the SYNTAX of a language, programming or human. It includes the parts of speech and the order in which they can be put together to create "correct" statements.

GRAPHICAL USER INTERFACE
See GUI.

GROUPWARE
SOFTWARE that helps a group of workers to share the knowledge needed to co-operate in doing their jobs. Probably today's leading exponent of the genre is a product from LOTUS DEVELOPMENT called Notes. At the heart of Notes are discussion

databases, which enable workers to share
information. The basic capabilities of these
databases are quite simple, but their impact on
business processes is potentially vast because they
enable workers to access simultaneously information which previously they could only hand on to
the next person in rigid sequence.

Notes databases are typically organised rather
like correspondence files. Under each subject
heading come various contributions, which will
include not only E-MAIL but also other electronic
documents including spreadsheets, DATABASE
reports and text from word processors.

Such information-sharing capabilities have
proved themselves useful in a variety of situations
where companies need to bring diverse skills and
knowledge to bear on a single task. Qantas uses
Notes to help marketing and operations work
together in devising flight schedules; Manufacturer's Hanover uses the technology to bring
together the pieces of giant international loans;
Lotus uses Notes to help sell Notes; and international management consultancies use the technology to capture the expertise of consulting teams
spread across the world.

But there is far more to groupware than Notes.
IBM and others offer rival discussion databases,
and there are other, more structured forms of the
technology, specialised to suit specific tasks.
Some products help a group of writers to manage
collaboration on a joint text; others work with
COMPUTER AIDED DESIGN systems to help engineers
work together on design projects. Meeting support software is designed to help groups of managers get the most out of meetings.

One of the problems with all of these forms of
electronic teamwork is that groups of people
interact differently when communicating electronically from when they are face-to-face. In general,
electronic communication is a leveller. For better
and worse, it breaks up the bonds of social hierarchy which hold groups together. It makes it easier to brainstorm but harder to reach consensus.
Many MEETING SUPPORT SYSTEMS rely on a human

facilitator to help to move groups towards agreement; in other applications groupware often accompanies a shift towards more independent, empowered styles of working. For having given workers all the information needed to make up their own minds, it is hard to stop them from doing so.

GSM

Abbreviation for Global System for Mobile communications, the European STANDARD for DIGITAL mobile telephones.

GUI

Short for Graphical User Interface, pronounced *goo-ey*. Strictly, a GUI is any computer that communicates with its user using pictures as well as words. In practice, most GUIS today build on work originated at Xerox's Palo Alto Research Center (PARC), which has four key elements.

- **WINDOW.** Instead of a single screen, the computer screen is separated into several different areas, each independent of the others. Each window might display a separate program, or a distinct view of the same program.
- **ICON.** Instead of describing programs and DATA with names, today's GUIS often use pictures. A WORD PROCESSOR might be represented by a pen, for example.
- **MOUSE.** Instead of typing commands to a program, GUIS enable a user to move a pointer, or CURSOR, around the screen using a device called a mouse.
- **MENU.** Instead of forcing the user to remember the handful of magic words which programs understand, GUIS present choices from a list of options (which typically appears in its own window on the screen).

The earliest popular computer to embody these ideas was APPLE'S MACINTOSH, which, when it appeared in 1984, was greatly inspired by visits to Xerox PARC. The Macintosh organises its screen as a virtual desktop. Files are represented as filing folders. Documents can be dropped into them for safe-keeping. Alternatively, files or folders can be dropped into a wastebasket for deletion. Since the Macintosh, similar ideas have been used to create interfaces for a variety of other systems, notably MICROSOFT'S WINDOWS for IBM-COMPATIBLE computers and X-WINDOWS for UNIX machines.

Two challenges will define the next generation of GUIS. The first is to represent active agents as well as passive objects like files. Particularly on big networks, a computer may be juggling several tasks at once, and new interfaces will have to keep users informed of the progress of all of them, interrupting if necessary yet not becoming intrusive.

The second challenge is to represent more and more complex data. The computer is no longer a window on to just the desktop, but on to the whole corporation and the world around it. Xerox PARC, for one, is now experimenting with three-dimensional interfaces which represent on the screen, say, the familiar corridors and layout of an executive's office building. For accounting information, the executive "walks" the screen to accounts, for marketing data to marketing, and so on. On Wall Street, by contrast, others are experimenting with the use of VIRTUAL-REALITY headsets to represent, in three-dimensional graphical glory, information which might help a securities trader to decide what is hot and what is not.

H

HACK
A neat piece of programming, often inspired by the need to solve or work around a specific problem. Also what a HACKER does.

HACKER
Strictly, a hacker is a skilled and dedicated programmer, who, in the words of *The New Hacker's Dictionary*, "enjoys exploring the details of programmable systems and how to stretch their capabilities, as opposed to most users, who prefer to learn only the minimum necessary". But the word has also recently come to connote a benign kind of computer prankster, dedicated to achieving unauthorised entry into, say, NASA's mission control computers, just to say he was there. (Contrast to CRACKER and PHREAKER.)

An experienced hacker was sitting next to a neophyte who was trying to fix his jammed terminal by turning the power off to reset the software. "Don't you know that you can't fix a computer just by cycling the power without knowing what's really going on?" said the hacker. Then he turned the power on and off, and the machine worked.

HALTING PROBLEM
One of the fundamental theories of computer science, the halting problem is not really a problem but refers to a proof which demonstrates the impossibility of creating a computer program which can determine whether any other program will eventually reach an answer. (Of course this is very easy for some programs, but not for all programs.) In effect, the halting problem is a demonstration that some things cannot be computed.

HANDSHAKE
A PROTOCOL used to co-ordinate the activities of two computers. Two computers might engage in a handshake to acknowledge each other's presence

---

H

on a NETWORK ("I'm here." "Yes, I see you; talk to you later.").

HANDWRITING RECOGNITION

Techniques for teaching a computer to read human handwriting. In theory, a computer should be able to analyse shapes and sequences of letters to guess words. In practice, most handwriting is sufficiently irregular to defeat that machine. By the mid-1990s the performance of handwriting recognition systems was the butt of many jokes, and the reason why PDAS did not live up to their initial hype, as the smart notebook which could fit into a jacket pocket.

HARD DISK

Or Winchester drive, after one of the inventors of the technology. This is a fixed, rigid DISK, typically permanently installed within a computer. Like a FLOPPY DISK, it is made by coating magnetic material on to a disk. But the rigid construction of hard disks means that they can be rotated more rapidly, and that DATA can be packed more precisely into smaller magnetic markings on the disk. Faster rotation means that data can be read and written more rapidly; more precise markings mean that more data can be packed on to the disk. By 1995 hard disks of 1 gigabyte were not uncommon; while most floppies held only about 1 megabyte, a difference of three orders of magnitude.

HARDWARE

Computer equipment that you can drop on your foot, assuming you could lift it in the first place. (Contrast to SOFTWARE.)

HEADER

DATA about data. Typically included at the beginning of a FILE, a document or a data PACKET sent over a communications NETWORK, the header typically contains information to identify the attached data, to state how much data is attached, what sort of data it is, how long it is and to help detect and/or correct errors.

HEISENBUG

A BUG (or defect) which is difficult to replicate or to diagnose. It is named after the Heisenberg Uncertainty Principle, which told physicists that there were limits to the accuracy with which they could measure the speed and momentum of an object: limits which only really matter at sub-atomic distances and speeds near that of light, but limits nonetheless. These limits arise because the very act of measuring an object disturbs it. Similarly, the act of observing a program in operation disturbs it.

HERTZ

A measure of FREQUENCY named after the German scientist Heinrich Hertz: one cycle per second.

HEURISTIC

A rule of thumb. It refers to computations which rely on human wisdom and experience to solve problems, rather than a formal, mathematically rigorous ALGORITHM. A rule-based EXPERT SYSTEM, for example, is commonly based on heuristics learned by interviewing human experts.

HEXADECIMAL

A number system which counts by 16s instead of the tens usual in the DECIMAL system. This is convenient for describing the contents of computer MEMORY, because two hexadecimal digits correspond to a single BYTE, in contrast to decimal numbers, which do not fit so neatly. Counting by 16s, however, requires new digits to represent the numbers 10–15, which is by convention done with the letters A–F. (See also BINARY.)

HIERARCHICAL DATABASE

A now largely outdated form of DATABASE which, as the name suggests, organises information in a hierarchy. If, for example, the database was to store information on the employees of the parks department, it might first categorise them by job: gardeners, street sweepers, tree surgeons, and so on. Then it might list names under each category, and addresses under each name, and so on.

This scheme of organisation turns out to be quite quick and easy for a computer to manage, and because of its speed the technology was adopted by many banks. But it also has two large drawbacks. First, it is quick only so long as the database is looking up information within a single hierarchy; finding a gardener's address, for example. It becomes very slow and clumsy when trying to compare the addresses of all employees. Worse, not all data are created equal. So if employees for some reason no longer fit into an established category – say because they are on sick leave – then they disappear from the database altogether. For these reasons the hierarchical database has largely been replaced by the RELATIONAL DATABASE.

HIGH ORDER
The most significant (those furthest to the left when the number is written out) BITS of a BINARY digit. As fiddling with the hundreds digit in 124 is a bigger change than fiddling with the ones, so changing the high order bits creates a bigger change than changing the LOW ORDER ones.

HOLLERITH CARD
A computing antique. The PUNCHED CARD was originally created for mechanical calculators built in the 1880s by Herman Hollerith. Hollerith also invented a special code for writing numbers on the cards, called, not surprisingly, the Hollerith code.

HOST COMPUTER
Strictly, the computer which holds the program and/or DATA under consideration. More generically, any big computer likely to hold a lot of programs and data. (See also CLIENT SERVER.)

HTML
Hypertext mark-up language, the programming language which creates the documents and links used by the WORLD WIDE WEB. The language con-

tains both commands for laying out text and graphics on a page, and also commands to link one document to another – or to link a document to an interactive computer program – to create HYPERMEDIA.

HUFFMAN CODING
A form of DATA COMPRESSION, which works on the quite reasonable principle that the most commonly used symbol should have the shortest code. So instead of, as ASCII does, giving all the characters of the alphabet seven-BIT codes, a Huffman code would make the letter e the shortest – at least for English in which it is the most common character.

HYPERMEDIA
Like HYPERTEXT, but including sound, video and other media.

HYPERTEXT
Text that need not be read from beginning to end, but can instead be browsed in any number of different orders, at the reader's whim, by following internal route-marks called links. A typical application of hypertext is in reference works, like this one. In an electronic version of this book, cross-references would not only be distinguished by special type, but they could also be "live". Click on them with a MOUSE and – whoosh – the computer brings up the appropriate entry on the screen.

Today's most popular application of hypertext (strictly speaking hypermedia) is the WORLD WIDE WEB, which uses the technology to link a vast collection of INFORMATION spread across the INTERNET. By clicking on highlighted words and pictures, net-surfers can call up a satellite photograph of the weather, or query a DATABASE of securities prices, or begin a global search for academic publications, or … well, you name it. But hypertext is also being used in a variety of other applications. Hypertext electronic reference works are becoming common, and many are experimenting with hypertext novels. For an interesting, if somewhat pretentious, techno-literary discussion, try debating at your next dinner party the proposition: "hypertext means the death of narrative".

HYPERTEXT MARK-UP LANGUAGE
See HTML.

IBM

The world's biggest computer company. IBM (International Business Machines) is the only computer company to compete globally in all sectors of the computer market, from the MAINFRAME to the PERSONAL COMPUTER (PC). Over the course of the 1970s and 1980s it grew to four or five times the size of its nearest competitors. Then, just when it seemed IBM could not help but take over the world, it ran into serious trouble.

For most of its history IBM has been run by marketers and salesmen. Thomas J. Watson Sr made his career and reputation as a salesman before he was appointed in 1914 to run the Computing-Tabulating-Recording Company, when it was renamed IBM, by a Wall Street financier, Charles Flint. His son followed his path through sales to the top of the rapidly expanding company. As it moved into computers in the 1950s and 1960s, IBM's focus on the customer helped it ease fears about the new technology, and gain the widespread trust needed to lead the market.

The product that brought IBM to the top of the computer market was System/360, launched in the early 1960s. The selling point of System/360 was simply that it offered a range of computers, from big to small, that could all run the same SOFTWARE and use the same DISK drives, printers and other peripherals. So a company could start with a small machine and work up to a large one as its needs grew, without investing in new software or accessories.

From System/360 to the launch of IBM's PC in 1981, technology advanced quickly enough to baffle even the most intrepid consumer. IBM salespeople prospered in part by providing reassurance. "You never get fired for buying IBM." That trust, in turn, generated so much cash that IBM's Thomas J. Watson research laboratories could spend more each year on research and development than many of its competitors chalked up in total sales. But, as is often the case, the seeds of trouble were being sown just as IBM seemed most invulnerable.

Three changes created a crisis at IBM by the early 1990s.

- **IBM-COMPATIBLE PCS.** When it launched its PC, IBM decided to buy its MICROPROCESSOR from INTEL and its OPERATING SYSTEM from MICROSOFT, and to use an easily copied BUS to link its computer together. Rivals could buy the same components. The result was copy-cat, IBM-compatible computers sold at cut prices by companies which did not have the overheads IBM had built up as it created the sales, marketing and support staff necessary to hold customers' hands. Although IBM's technology accounted for nearly 90% of personal computers sold, IBM itself made only just over 10%.

- **Technological complexity.** By the late 1980s IBM was increasingly hard-pressed to make good its promise to make the right technological choices for its customers. There were simply too many technologies for IBM salespeople to stay on top of, particularly as the company felt obliged to support its own aged machines as well as the new ones coming on to the market. Customers began to complain that they were being sold what was most convenient for IBM rather than what was best for them. The managerial procedures that IBM put into place to help support sales staff slowed down decision-making, which caused further dissatisfaction.

- **Customer sophistication.** As computers spread across corporate desktops, and the ability to purchase PCs fell within even modest budgets, more and more managers became comfortable with the idea of making their own decisions about computers (sometimes unrealistically comfortable). So customers began to look more critically at IBM's judgements just as technological complexity made it more difficult for IBM to make good ones.

Such changes threw IBM into disarray. Market

share was falling, and it made huge losses. Executives were talking about breaking the company up into smaller, more manageable units. For the first time since Thomas J. Watson Sr began to build the firm, IBM brought in an outsider as chairman: Louis Gerstener, a former executive of American Express who was then running RJR Nabisco. He shelved plans to break up the firm, and began trying to find ways of combining the strength and resources of a giant firm with the nimbleness and entrepreneurial independence of a small one. The crisis passed, but the struggle will be a long one.

IBM-COMPATIBLE

A PERSONAL COMPUTER built to run the same SOFTWARE, and accept the same HARDWARE add-ons, as IBM's personal computers. This typically means an INTEL MICROPROCESSOR, MICROSOFT'S DOS and WINDOWS operating systems and a PCI or an ISA BUS to link the parts together (although EISA and MCA buses are also used).

In the 1992–93 school year, 64% of the computers used in American schools were Apple IIs and only 25% were IBMS and IBM-compatibles.

ICON

A graphic device, designed to make a program or FILE quickly and easily recognisable on a computer screen. What mice usually click on.

IDENTITY HACKING

Pretending to be someone else on a computer NETWORK. (After all, if nobody can see your face, why not?) For reasons best left to their psychiatrists, many men seem to enjoy pretending to be women on computer networks, particularly in conversations where sex is involved.

IMPLEMENTATION

A real working piece of HARDWARE or SOFTWARE, as opposed to an abstract specification, sometimes used in contrast to INTERFACE.

I

INDUCTION

A way of reasoning about the properties of things which can be counted, or at least arranged in a sequence. Proofs by induction typically involve two steps. First prove that the first element of the sequence has the property in question. Then show that if some arbitrary element of the sequence has the property, the next element in the sequence must also have the property. If so, hey presto, all the elements of the sequence must have the property. (The first one has it, and if the first one has it then the second one has it, and if the second one has it then the third one has it, and so on.)

INFOMATION

A term coined by Soshana Zuboff, in her book *The Age of the Smart Machine*, to try to distinguish the impact of computers from traditional AUTOMATION. The key difference is the amount of INFORMATION each makes available to workers.

Automation disenfranchises workers because it breaks work down into a rigidly defined series of small steps, and, as it does so, it makes it hard for workers performing their tasks to comprehend the rest of the process. The use of computers, Soshana Zuboff argues, can (but does not always) eliminate these barriers. Sometimes inadvertently, computers enable workers to see beyond their own tasks, and to comprehend the process as a whole. At the same time, the flexibility of computer technology can enable a more flexible, ad hoc division of labour to substitute for the rigid, fixed divisions of the production line. GROUPWARE tries to make the most of the opportunities for new styles of working which computers can create.

INFORMATION

Nobody has yet managed to give a really precise definition of information, which is somewhat odd considering that we are in the middle of an information revolution and more and more of the world's population are now earning their living from the stuff. Instinctively, information is useful

DATA; that is, it is data that answers questions instead of just taking up space. But pinning down more precisely the notion of "useful" has proved tricky.

The first rigorous definition of information was created by Claude Shannon of AT&T's Bell Labs in 1948. It is in many ways a mathematical version of an old newspaperman's saying: "Dog bites man is not news; but man bites dog is." The reason why, says Shannon, is that the information carried by an event is directly proportional to the probability of its occurring. Expected events carry little information; unexpected ones carry a lot.

Shannon used this insight to calculate the amounts of information carried by communication lines under various conditions, and to get a grip on how NOISE on the line, by obscuring parts of the signal, can reduce information-carrying capacity. But Shannon's theory has big limitations, as he himself was the first to admit. Because it relies so heavily on the probability of forthcoming events, it is impossible to cope with the myriad shades of meaning. Instead it views the world in terms of symbols in a communications channel, like the letters on this page. (Shannon went on to do work on the amount of information carried by the letters of written English, and, perhaps unsurprisingly, found that there were large amounts of redundancy coded into the language, often in the final letters of a word, which no longer help to distinguish it from others but which we write anyway.)

Although still influential, Shannon's view of information has in some applications been superseded by an algorithmic view of information. As the name implies, this theory views information in terms of algorithms. Specifically, it argues that the amount of information carried by an event is directly proportional to the smallest computer program which could reproduce the event (given some idealised computer).

Everybody gets so much information all day long that they lose their common sense.
Gertrude Stein

INFORMATION HIGHWAY
Nickname for the world's growing collection of
BROADBAND communications networks.

*Information wants to be free; it also wants
to be expensive.*
Steward Brand

INFORMATION RETRIEVAL
The task of searching for INFORMATION by subject
or topic. Getting a computer to look up information relevant to some given topic turns out to be a
far trickier task than it first seems. A large part of
the problem lies in the sheer slipperiness of information. If you knew what you were looking
for, you would not need to ask the computer.

Over the years computer scientists and librarians have devised several approaches to the problem, including the following.

- **Full-text search.** Computers can speed
  through the complete text of documents to
  find given words. The snag, however, is that
  such a search will often return hundreds or
  thousands of documents.
- **KEYWORD search.** Many books and papers are
  now filed by a list of words denoting the
  most important topics covered. This works
  but requires great skill and consistency on
  the part of the people classifying the documents.
- **Probabilistic searching.** This technique
  searches the full text of a document for a list of
  words. But not all matches are treated equally.
  Matches to words that occur infrequently in
  the overall collection of documents are considered more important than those that occur
  frequently in ranking matches.
- **Relevance feedback.** Having found one
  document that contains interesting stuff, this
  technique uses information from that document – keywords, infrequently occurring
  words, or whatever – to refine the search.

- **Parsing.** Some programs try to use ARTIFICIAL INTELLIGENCE to understand the text more or less as humans do. While the approach is instinctively appealing, there is no evidence that it performs better than statistical techniques.

INK-JET PRINTER

A PRINTER which forms letters by shooting tiny droplets of ink on to the page. The heart of an ink-jet printer is a cleverly designed nozzle and ink cartridge. One wall of the ink cartridge oscillates rapidly as an electric current is passed through it, forcing a steady stream of tiny droplets out of the nozzle. On leaving the nozzle, the droplets pass through a precisely varied magnetic field, which deflects them to just the right spot on the page to form the next tiny addition to the letter or drawing under construction. Ink-jet printers offer quality of printing nearly as good as a LASER PRINTER, but for less money. They can also work on surfaces which laser printers cannot cope with, such as cloth or, in one entrepreneur's dream, cakes and other food.

INSTRUCTION SET

The complete collection of all the nouns and verbs in the assembly language for a particular MICROPROCESSOR. As the instruction set defines the basic capabilities of the chip, it determines which sorts of programs are easy to write and which are hard. In the 1970s chip designers tried to include more and more capabilities in the instruction set. In the 1980s, however, most decided that the extra complexity of large instruction sets was not worth the convenience. Most modern chips are therefore built on the principles of reduced instruction set computing or RISC.

INTEGER

A whole number, like 1, 2 or 3, but not 1.5 or 6.54, which are real numbers but not integers. Hence calculations performed only with integers are referred to as integer arithmetic. (See also REAL NUMBER.)

INTEGRATED SERVICES DIGITAL NETWORK
See ISDN.

INTEL
The company which invented the MICROPROCESSOR.
Unlike many SEMICONDUCTOR innovators, which
have seen their innovations gain commercial glory
in the hands of rivals, Intel has dominated the
microprocessor sector for nearly two decades.

Intel was founded by Robert Noyce, Andy
Grove and other engineers who broke away from
Fairchild Semiconductor, the firm which was the
grandfather of both commercial innovation in
semiconductors and Silicon Valley entrepreneur-
ialism. Its early products were mostly computer
MEMORY chips, but in 1968 one of its engineers,
Ted Hoff, realised that advances in the miniatur-
isation of circuitry enabled him to fit on to a single piece of silicon all of the components of a
computer's CPU (that is, its calculating engine).
Thus the microprocessor was born.

Because of the performance trade-offs in mini-
aturisation, Intel had to struggle to sell early
microprocessors. Its first customer was a Japanese
firm which used the device to build a pocket calculator. In 1980, however, IBM chose Intel's 8088
microprocessor to power its entry in the PERSONAL
COMPUTER market and a *de facto* STANDARD was set.
Although Intel was driven out of the mainstream
memory chip business by fierce Japanese competition in the early 1980s, its microprocessors
have gone from strength to strength.

Intel's microprocessors now power over 80% of
the personal computers sold in the world. Its
dominance is buttressed by the millions of SOFT-
WARE packages written to run on its microprocessors, which would have to be adapted or rewritten
for any competitor who hoped to usurp Intel's
role. The fifth generation of Intel microprocessors
was called the Pentium after Intel discovered that
its tradition of numbering chips (8088, 80286,
80386, 80486) rendered the names unprotectable
by either copyright or trademark.

INTERFACE

The technology needed to get two computer and/or communication systems to work together. It is where things usually go wrong.

In the vocabulary of open systems, engineers increasingly make a distinction between interface and IMPLEMENTATION. Interfaces are abstract, commonly agreed, public standards, available to everybody. Implementations turn interfaces into real working programs, and are the source of proprietary competitive advantage.

INTERNATIONAL STANDARDS ORGANISATION

See ISO.

From November 1992 to November 1994 the number of messages sent over the Internet grew fourfold, to over 1 trillion a month.

INTERNET

The world's largest computer NETWORK, which by 1995 linked about 5m computers and tens of millions of people – and was still growing at 50-100% a year. The Internet has managed this growth because it is a new kind of infrastructure, built to mutually agreed technical standards, largely with private capital and effort and from the bottom up.

Nobody is in charge of the Internet; its size is measured simply by sending out a query from a computer in California and asking all machines that receive the message to reply. Its technical standards are all voluntarily, although those who do not wish to abide by them will simply not be able to communicate with their fellows. Connecting to the Internet is nearly as simple as renting a connection to somebody else on the Internet; there is a minimum of bureaucracy and administration.

Like any computer network the Internet is defined by the answers to two questions: Who talks to whom? and How do they do it? Technically, the answer to the first question concerns addresses. Each computer on the Internet is given both a name (for people to use) and a number (for other machines to use). Translation between names and numbers is automatic, and the organisation of addresses reflects the overall organisation of the network.

Like street addresses, each Internet address reflects a hierarchy. To deliver a letter to St James's Street, London, the post office might first send the letter to the London sorting office and then let it find the proper street. So too with delivering E-MAIL to *jb@zeno.somewhere.uk*. To the Internet-savvy, this message denotes a person called *jb*, at a machine called *zeno* in the domain *somewhere.uk*. Like paper mail, the message can first be delivered to the computer managing the *somewhere.uk* domain, and then that computer can find the machine called *zeno*.

This hierarchy of responsibilities is one of the keys to the Internet's fast growth. It makes its complexity manageable by devolving responsibility for each system to the lowest possible point. To a large extent, each of the many networks which make up the Internet can hide its internal workings from the others. It is up to individual network administrators to choose how, and how much, they want the machines in their domain to participate in the larger life of the network.

At the most basic level, the Internet offers three ways for the people and machines it connects to communicate.

- **E-MAIL.** Many big ON-LINE services, like CompuServe and America On-Line, offer their customers only e-mail connections to the Internet. E-mail accounts for about a tenth of Internet traffic, the third largest share.
- **TELNET.** Using this service, a person on one computer connected to the Internet can log-in to another computer on the net and use its services as if it were sitting at his or her desk.
- **FTP.** This service transmits bulk DATA across the Internet and accounts for the largest single share of Internet traffic (about a third).

From the very beginning, one of the purposes of the Internet was to support research into networking technology. So the Internet is continually evolving. New services like the WORLD WIDE WEB make the Internet almost as easy to use as pointing and clicking on a MACINTOSH computer. In just a few years the ease and speed with which the Web can serve up information from around the world has made it the second-largest source of traffic over the Internet. Meanwhile, experiments are being made in creating a more interactive network, with videoconferencing and the network equivalent of voice telephone calls.

For the future, some of the most vexing issues concerning the Internet are cultural rather than technical. With growth, the Internet now reaches far beyond the basement rooms of university computing science departments. Some see its tens of millions of users as a market ripe for plucking. But there are, as yet, no commonly accepted rules of behaviour, or NETIQUETTE, for advertising on the Internet. Nor are there yet in place many of the SECURITY mechanisms, like PUBLIC-KEY CRYPTOGRAPHY, needed to move cash over the Internet without risk of theft. But given its astonishing growth in the past, there is no reason to think that these problems will slow the Internet's breakneck growth any more than the seemingly intractable problems it has already overcome.

> *The Coca-Cola machine at Carnegie Mellon University in Pittsburgh is connected to the Internet. To find out how many cokes it holds type finger coke@cs.cmu.edu.*

INTERNET PROTOCOL
The IP in TCP/IP, these are the technical standards which specify how packets on the INTERNET are routed from one machine to another. Each PACKET travels independently, and packets may follow very different routes. In terms of the SEVEN LAYER REFERENCE MODEL, IP is the NETWORK layer of the Internet.

> *The Net interprets censorship as damage, and routes around it.*
> John Gilmore

INTERNETWORKING

A generic term used to describe the process of linking together different networks – as is done, for example, in the INTERNET (and from which the Internet took its name).

INTER-OPERABILITY

Like STANDARD, inter-operability is rapidly becoming one of the more meaningless words in information technology. When technology companies talk about inter-operable systems, they imply that the systems can easily be made to work together. But there are a wide variety of different interpretations of what "easily" might mean in this context. *Caveat emptor.*

INTERPRETER

A piece of SOFTWARE which understands and executes programs written in high-level languages like BASIC, LISP and PROLOG. In contrast to a COMPILER, an interpreter executes the statements of these languages directly, without the initial step to translate them into MACHINE CODE. The extra effort required for on-the-fly translation means that interpreted programs run more slowly than compiled ones. But they are faster and easier to DEBUG. Many languages for experimental programming, like LISP and Prolog (widely used in ARTIFICIAL INTELLIGENCE), are interpreted. Languages for production systems, like C, C++ and COBOL, are typically compiled.

INTERRUPT

A way of handling unpredictable events within a computer, like the press of a key on a keyboard, or the arrival of a message over a NETWORK. As the name suggests, an interrupt forces the MICROPROCESSOR to drop what it is doing and deal with the new event, after which it can go back to work as normal. Interrupts are used as an alternative to POLLING, where the microprocessor continually asks the keyboard (or the network port, or whatever) if they have any work that needs doing. The advantage of interrupts is that they do not waste time looking for work when there is none to do; the disadvantage is the complexity and potential difficulties of making sure that, even if an interrupt occurs when least expected (as they inevitably seem to do), the computer can happily resume work as normal.

IO

Computer shorthand for input-output; that is, the work of getting DATA into the computer and back out again. These are by far the most time consuming and tricky jobs in computing. In part because most must interact mechanically with the real world, IO devices work more slowly than the whizzing of electrons within CPUs. So, in practice, most programs spend most of their time waiting for input or output; they are, in the vernacular, IO-bound. MULTI-TASKING operating systems were originally created to take advantage of these delays, by allowing another program to use the CPU while its predecessor waited for IO and then reverting to the original program when IO finished.

IP

See INTERNET PROTOCOL.

ISA

Short for Industry Standard Architecture, the BUS used to link the MICROPROCESSOR and other HARDWARE of IBM's original PERSONAL COMPUTER. Although widely copied, it is now rivalled by faster, more powerful PCI, EISA and MCA buses.

ISDN

Abbreviation for Integrated Services Digital Network, the next generation of higher-BANDWIDTH, DIGITAL communications services. Not only is ISDN a digital service, which offers better error correction than today's ANALOGUE telephone services, but it also offers at least twice the bandwidth of existing analogue services. However, as the name implies, the key difference between ISDN and plain old telephone service (POTS) is that it accepts the fact that, in the modern world, voices will share the line with a number of other services.

ISO
The International Standards Organisation, a STAN-DARD-setting body which has created the SEVEN LAYER REFERENCE MODEL, a widely used way of categorising different sorts of communications capabilities, among other standards.

J

JANET

Acronym for Joint Academic Network, the UK's version of the USA's INTERNET. A recent, higher-BANDWIDTH version of JANET is called SuperJANET.

JCL

Short for Job Control Language, a programming language used in IBM mainframes and notorious for its awkwardness and insistence on obscure points of SYNTAX. While most languages will, for example, happily allow two or more spaces where they expected one, JCL insists that one and only one is right, and anything else is unacceptable.

JOB

As in normal usage, a task for a computer to do.

JOIN

The fundamental technique for relating fragments of DATA stored in a RELATIONAL DATABASE. Relational databases store information in tables, and, to ease management, designers try to keep tables small and simple. So how do you ask a complicated question? With a join.

Say a computer shopkeeper had a database containing one table with the names and addresses of customers, and another with a record of what each customer bought, indexed by name. To send a mailing to all of those who have bought Brand X computers, the shopkeeper must do a join on the two tables to associate the addresses of Brand X buyers with the information about their computing preferences. To be joined, tables must obviously share an index (in this case, the name of the customer). Then it is relatively straightforward to marry up the information in one to that of the other.

JPEG

Joint Picture Experts Group, referring to standards for the COMPRESSION and format of DIGITAL images. JPEG files are pictures stored digitally in the JPEG format. MPEG is roughly the same, but for moving pictures.

K

An abbreviation for KILO, as in 256k MEMORY chip.

KERBEROS

A set of protocols developed at the Massachusetts Institute of Technology to maintain security in distributed systems. Kerberos ensures that users can gain access to only those files and computing services to which they have been granted access by the systems administrator. In a distributed computing environment, where users regularly move from machine to machine and new services are regularly being added, this is a lot harder than it sounds.

KERMIT

A communications program often used to send DATA between personal computers and larger machines. It comes with its own, eponymous PROTOCOL for detecting and correcting errors. Both program and protocol were developed at Columbia University and named after the frog on *Sesame Street*, a children's television programme.

KERNEL

The heart of a MULTI-TASKING OPERATING SYSTEM. One of the key design challenges in creating an operating system that will allow several users to share the same machine is to make sure that one program cannot mess up another's work, even if that program was created by a user who maliciously wishes to do so. This requires a benevolent dictator to manage all of the programs working on the machine: sharing out time on the CPU, making sure that two programs do not try to use the PRINTER at the same time, and so on. That benevolent dictator is the kernel.

In recent years a trend in operating systems has been to reduce the size of the kernel – to create micro-kernels – by building into the kernel only a very few, but powerful functions. Programs do not interact with the micro-kernel directly, but through an intermediary. The hope is that by building clever intermediaries, systems developers might enable operating systems to take on different personalities, with the same underlying microkernel appearing through one intermediary as, say, IBM's OS/2 operating system and through another as UNIX.

KEY

The information used to decode an encrypted message. Traditionally key management, getting keys from the person sending the encoded message to the person who is to decode it, has been the hardest part of managing secure cryptography. If any key fell into the wrong hands, the SECURITY of the whole system was compromised. That has changed, however, with the advent of PUBLIC-KEY CRYPTOGRAPHY. This technique splits keys into two parts: a public one, which can be advertised for anyone wishing to encode a message to, say, Phil Zimmerman, and a private key, which Phil can use to decode any message encoded with his public key.

KEYWORD

A word used as a tag or marker for INFORMATION RETRIEVAL. Keywords say what a book, article or other piece of text is about. They are typically abstracted by professional librarians, who read the text and then annotate it with the words which they think best describe its content. It is then easy to use a computer to search for articles whose keywords match the subjects of interest to some inquiring mind. The problem with keywords, however, is the difficulty of maintaining consistency and accuracy when different articles are read, classified and searched for by different librarians. One librarian's "information technology" maybe another's "computer science".

KILL

To stop a program from running. Most operating systems provide kill commands which can be typed at the keyboard to stop unwanted programs, even if some BUG has stopped the program from responding to its usual command to quit. In

UNIX the command is quite appropriately called kill.

KILL FILE
A way of filtering out annoying messages from a USENET NEWS GROUP and other electronic forums. Even in an otherwise interesting subject, some people and/or topics can become so annoying that you never want to see them again. Kill files offer a way of making sure that you don't. By entering a name, subject or other distinguishing feature of the unwanted messages into the kill file, SOFTWARE can automatically delete the potentially offending messages before they are read. Ignorance is then bliss. On some systems kill files are also called bozo filters.

KILO
Strictly, the prefix denotes a thousand, but as the computer world counts in twos rather than tens it is here used to refer to 1,024 (2^{10}).

KLUGE
Pronounced *klooj*, from the German for clever; a too-clever programming trick. Like a HACK, but generally used with an element of disdain to denote work that is either an obviously temporary fix or else over-elaborate.

KNOWLEDGE ENGINEERING
The process of extracting the knowledge of a human expert for use in building a computerised EXPERT SYSTEM.

> *Where is the knowledge that is lost in information? Where is the wisdom that is lost in knowledge?*
> T. S. Eliot

LAMBDA CALCULUS

A theory of calculation created by a mathematician, Alonzo Church. The lambda calculus enables mathematicians to prove results about what can and cannot be calculated. It also provided inspiration for the programming language LISP.

LAN

See LOCAL AREA NETWORK.

LANGUAGE UNDERSTANDING

There are two parts to the task of teaching a computer to talk. The first is to recognise words, and the second to understand them. When words are written, recognising words is easy. But speech requires more effort.

Linguists have long known that all words are composed of a handful of basic sounds, called phonemes, strung together in different combinations. In theory, then, recognising a spoken word should be little harder than recognising a written one – just keep track of the sequence of phonemes. The snag, however, is that various phonemes sound different in different contexts. The same phoneme can be pronounced differently by different people. The same person can pronounce them differently depending on whether he is asking a question or making a statement. Worst of all, people often do not pause between words as meticulously as they put spaces in sentences.

So recognising spoken language requires statistical models which make educated guesses about which words and phonemes they might be hearing – and constantly refine those guesses as each new sound is heard. Given training to accustom them to the voice of a particular speaker, some such systems can take dictation consisting of thousands of different words. But if they must cope with any speaker, performance falls dramatically. AT&T has been experimenting with replacing some of its long-distance telephone operators with a system that can understand the ten digits, yes, no, and little else.

L

Given words, the harder task is to make sense of them. Here the problem is mostly the sheer amount of knowledge required to disentangle even a seemingly simple sentence. For example, the sentence "The turkeys are ready to eat" has two entirely different meanings – one for the Christmas table and one for the barnyard. To distinguish one from the other requires more than just the meanings of the words; it also requires a lot of the common-sense knowledge that people take for granted, but which computers lack utterly. Although computers are beginning to do simple things with language – like routing incoming telexes at banks – real understanding is a long, long way off.

LASER PRINTER
A PRINTER which creates high-quality, near-typeset printing by using a laser beam to etch characters. The laser beam creates small changes in the electrical field on a large, smooth drum. Where the beam has changed the field, toner sticks to the drum, which is then heated and pressed on to paper to print.

LAST IN, FIRST OUT
See LIFO.

LEASED LINE
A way of buying bulk telecommunications BANDWIDTH. Instead of paying the NETWORK provider by the minute, a leased line provides some fixed amount of capacity for a flat annual fee, which must be paid whether the line is used or not. Leasing capacity is in most countries more economic for firms that transmit lots of DATA, but costs vary widely from nation to nation.

LED
See LIGHT-EMITTING DIODE.

LEGACY SYSTEM
An ageing computer system, usually on a MAINFRAME, often one which inhibits corporate change.

L

In many companies legacy systems dominate the IT-management agenda. They are often difficult both to modify and to replace. They are written in programming languages never encountered by programmers under the age of 40, and years of haphazard modification have made the code both obscure and fragile. Even seemingly innocuous changes can simply break the program. Yet legacy systems often perform crucial corporate functions, like accounts receivable or inventory management.

IT managers have developed several different approaches to updating legacy systems.

- **Scrap them.** Some systems are simply so old and flaky that there is no alternative but to rebuild them from scratch.
- **Wrap them.** Some legacy systems work perfectly well, but they employ technologies that work awkwardly with modern networks and CLIENT-SERVER systems, so companies are building wrappers which can intermediate between old and new. So-called hub SOFTWARE enables old legacy systems to communicate over modern networks, and it can seamlessly gather together DATA scattered across several databases to answer a single query (which is useful in the modern managerial pursuit of building cross-functional processes). Another technology, called object wrappers, can enable legacy systems, or components of legacy systems, to work with modern object-oriented software.
- **Convert them.** Software exists, particularly for ageing databases, that can take data from an outdated DATABASE and recast it in the format required by a new RELATIONAL DATABASE.

The really hard question for managers to ask themselves, however, is how to prevent today's new systems from becoming tomorrow's legacies. Depressingly, that is a question with more good ideas than solid answers.

LIFO

Last In, First Out, an approach to managing incoming and outgoing DATA. LIFO dictates that the most recently arrived piece of data will be the next to be used. Although this changes the order of the data in ways that depend somewhat unpredictably on the timing of arrivals and departures, it turns out to be convenient for many computing applications. A commonly used form of LIFO BUFFER is called a STACK.

LIGHT-EMITTING DIODE

A diode that glows when a current is passed through it. Light-emitting diodes (LEDs) are typically used in circuits to show if a piece of machinery, such as a disk drive, is on or off.

LINEAR PROGRAMMING

Describes computer programs concerned with minimisation or maximisation. As the name suggests, linear programming techniques can cope only with formulae which describe linear costs, values or whatever; that is, whose values per unit are constant. (The cost of a telephone call, for example, is linear because, typically, calls are charged at so much a minute – so the total cost of any call is simply a multiple of the per-minute charge.) With the constraint that the values involved be linear, and powerful computers, linear programming methods can find the highest-value, lowest-cost or otherwise best way of approaching problems described even by large collections of formulae. The most commonly used form of linear programming is called the SIMPLEX ALGORITHM.

LINK

A connection between two items of HYPERTEXT. In some hypertext systems links can be labelled to make explicit the relationship they denote. So one link might be labelled "supporting argument" and another "contrary argument". In theory, labels make it easier to solve the perennial problem of hypertext links, which is maintaining a sense of direction in the sea of INFORMATION. In practice, adding more information (on the labels) to all that is already there can easily be mishandled to create more confusion.

LINKER

A piece of SOFTWARE which assembles the components of a program for execution. Programs are typically written as a collection of subroutines, each of which does a specific task. In order to execute a SUBROUTINE, however, the computer must know where it is located in MEMORY. This is usually not known when the program is translated into MACHINE CODE during compilation; so the COMPILER leaves markers wherever it needs to call a subroutine, labelled, in effect, "wherever subroutine X may be". The linker then fills in the blanks.

LISP

An acronym derived from List Processing, a FUNCTIONAL PROGRAMMING language created by John McCarthy, a computer scientist at Stanford University, and widely used in ARTIFICIAL INTELLIGENCE. True to its name, LISP – and the functional programming traditions of the LAMBDA CALCULUS which inspired it – views the world in terms of lists and functions. This turns out to be remarkably convenient, once you get the hang of it.

LOADER

A piece of SOFTWARE which loads programs into MEMORY for execution. On an old-time MAINFRAME this was a separate program. On today's computers the task is handled by the OPERATING SYSTEM. But the name lingers on.

LOCAL AREA NETWORK

A DATA NETWORK that links nearby computers, typically in the same room, or at least in the same building. Today's most common local area networks are ETHERNET and TOKEN RING. On the horizon, however, are faster networks based on fibre optics, including FDDI.

LOCAL LOOP

Strictly, the link between a customer's telephone (or FAX machine, or MODEM, or whatever) and the nearest telephone switch. In practice, the term is loosely used to refer to the business of providing communications service to the end user. One of the interesting developments of coming years will be the growth of competition in the local loop, and the choices people will have to make about how to communicate with their peers.

Indeed, regulators permitting, tomorrow's homes and businesses could choose between as many as five different networks, each striving to serve them.

- **POTS** (plain old telephone service), although instead of today's relatively low BANDWIDTH telephone service, tomorrow's telephone companies will provide at least ISDN, and perhaps even higher bandwidth voice and DATA services.
- **Cable television.** In some parts of both the UK and the USA, cable television companies are offering telephone service as well as entertainment. Having laid the cables to carry television, there is little additional cost in adding telephone service over the same infrastructure.
- **Electric utilities.** With electric wires to every home and office, electric utilities already have the rights of way needed to offer telephone service. They would have to install extra equipment, but the cost of this equipment could be at least partially covered by the savings that more communication could bring in the utilities' own operations.
- **PERSONAL COMMUNICATIONS NETWORK.** In theory, new technology could enable the creation of low-cost cellular networks which offer a bandwidth somewhat greater than today's telephone services – although somewhat less than tomorrow's – at highly competitive costs. Better still, being wireless, they would also be mobile; the telephone would

live in your pocket, not on your desk.

- **Fixed cellular.** Perhaps using bandwidth freed when today's ANALOGUE television broadcasters shrink their signals into an efficiently compressed DIGITAL form, a second group of wireless communications companies may compete directly with wire-based services by offering radio-based communications via a transceiver attached to the side of the building. It would not be mobile, but it could be cheap.

The introduction of competition into the local loop presents a difficult problem for regulators. Having witnessed how competition has reduced costs while boosting quality in long-distance communications, many countries now wish to unleash potential competition in the local loop. But it is more difficult here to ensure that competition is fair, and that incumbent companies do not make it hard for their competitors to woo potential customers. Many regulators are also worried about the impact of competition on UNIVERSAL SERVICE.

Rate regulation has in the past forced telephone companies to provide residential telephone service at a loss. Although there is surprisingly little hard evidence about the size of this loss (or whether there still need be a loss given modern technology and proper accounting procedures) most regulators assume that they will need to find some way to continue to subsidise residential telephone rates even as they introduce competition, lest people find the price of communications moving beyond their reach as its importance for their well-being increases. Given that competition and subsidies coexist uneasily, universal service augments the regulators' challenge.

LOCK

A way of preventing conflict between two programs which might otherwise simultaneously try to use the same FILE, PRINTER or other resource. Before using the resource, programs check to see if some other program has "locked" access to it,

which is often done by creating a specially named
file on the DISK. If the lock exists, the program will
wait until the owner of the lock has finished; if it
does not, the program will create its own lock file
before proceeding.

LOG ON

To begin using a computer, a process which usually requires entering your name and PASSWORD at
the keyboard. Hence "log-on prompt", which is
what appears on the computer display after you
have successfully logged on. Log in is of course
the same thing with different words.

LOGIC

A formal method of reasoning. Informally, the
term is used to describe choices and calculations
made by a program, or to distinguish circuits
which calculate, like a MICROPROCESSOR, from those
which merely regurgitate, like MEMORY. More
strictly, logic describes a mathematical system of
DEDUCTION, which uses strict rules of reasoning to
determine the truth or falsity of statements.

Many of the rules of deduction of formal logic
are built into the connectives: and, or, not, and so
on. For example, the statement "A and B" is true if
and only if the statement A is true and the statement B is true; while "A or B" is true if either is
true, and "not A" is true if and only if A is false. So
"Lucy is a girl and Lucy is a boy" is necessarily
false (for people, at least), while "Lucy is a girl or
Lucy is a boy" is necessarily true.

Similar rules apply to logic circuits on chips. An
"and" circuit is on if all of its inputs are on; an "or"
circuit is on if one or more of its inputs is on; and
so on.

Leaving circuits aside, formal, mathematically
rigorous logic comes in several forms. Some of the
most commonly used are as follows.

- **Propositional logic.** The simplest useful
  logic, propositional logic talks about the truth
  or falsity of statements using and, or, not, and
  so on.

- **First-order logic.** To the basic capabilities of propositional logic, first-order logic adds the ability to talk about variables, that is things whose identity is not known in advance. Such variables can be universally quantified, which is to say that everything that that variable might stand for must have some property (say, be red in colour). Or they can be existentially quantified, which is to say that there must exist something which that variable stands for, and which has the given property.
- **Modal logic.** While most logic talks about things that are once and forever true or false – that circles are round, for example – modal logic provides extra mechanisms for reasoning about things that might change, for example the idea that Caesar is dead (for he wasn't always so).

Logic: the art of thinking and reasoning in strict accordance with the limitations and incapacities of the human understanding.
Ambrose Bierce, *The Devil's Dictionary*

LOGIC PROGRAMMING

Describes a family of DECLARATIVE PROGRAMMING languages which compute using rules very similar to LOGIC. Probably the most popular logic programming language is Prolog, created by Alain Colmerauer at the University of Marseille and Robert Kowalski, then at the University of Edinburgh, now at Imperial College, London.

Their insight was that the rules of logic specified a kind of programming language. Given statements of the form "X is a mammal if X is a dog" and "Y is warm-blooded if Y is a mammal", and a DATABASE naming several particular dogs, a computer could automatically deduce various facts about their blood temperature. (More rules make a program more useful.) Better still, it could do so without forcing the programmer to specify in tedious detail how the DEDUCTION was to be managed. So, in theory at least, programs could be written by specifying facts and logical rules of deduction, not machine mumbo-jumbo. The snag with this vision, however, is that some rules of deduction are easier for the computer to manage than others. Thus in practice the programmer cannot actually ignore the underlying technical details of how the language works without risking unpleasant surprises.

LOOP
One of the most commonly used constructs in computer programming, a loop is a series of instructions that repeats until some condition is met: perhaps all the characters in a FILE have been processed, or the loop has been repeated 100 times. A common programming error is to write a loop whose exit condition will never be met, in which case the loop will repeat endlessly until the program is killed. This is called an infinite loop. Not coincidentally, the street on which is located the headquarters of APPLE Computer is called Infinite Loop. But none of the programmers seem to mind having an address named after a mistake.

LOTUS DEVELOPMENT
The company that created Lotus 1-2-3, a best-selling SPREADSHEET for IBM-COMPATIBLE computers which made the machines seem indispensable on every executive desktop.

LZW ALGORITHM
The Lempel-Zev-Welch ALGORITHM is one of the most effective techniques for DATA COMPRESSION. It builds up a dictionary of sequences of characters with each entry numbered. When a previously encountered sequence is met again the number is substituted for the characters. The cleverness lies in the algorithm doing this coding so that the receiving program can decode and decompress the data as easily as the encoding one can compress it.

M

M
An abbreviation for MEGA, as in 1M MEMORY chip.

MACHINE CODE
A synonym for ASSEMBLY LANGUAGE.

MACHINE LEARNING
The process of teaching a computer new tricks. To some extent, machines can be taught more or less like people: by showing them examples of what is right and what is wrong and allowing them to compare. But computers are much stupider than people, and in particular they have little idea of what concepts might be relevant to a specific problem. So a perennial struggle for those who would teach computers is to focus the machine's attention on the specific features of a problem that differentiate a right example from a wrong one. A square is not different from a circle because you only see one when it is dark outside, although a computer which had only seen circles at night would be quite happy to believe so.

One way of overcoming this problem is to construct carefully the examples used in teaching, so that each differs from the others by only one or two significant features. Another way for computers to learn is for them to try to fit each example into a set of ready-made templates, or explanations, with a human to correct them when the explanations go wrong. Yet another way is for the machine simply to serve as a memory aide, indexing all of the situations it has encountered so that a person can more easily retrieve the experience of situations similar to the one at hand (see CASE-BASED REASONING). Finally, both the GENETIC ALGORITHM and the NEURAL NET in some sense learn by adapting to their environment.

MACINTOSH
APPLE's flagship computer, the Macintosh revolutionised computing by bringing the easy-to-use, graphical user interface (GUI) to the desktop, popularising ideas developed at Xerox's Palo Alto Research Center. The Macintosh was the first

popular computer sold with a MOUSE; it was the first to use a MENU-DRIVEN INTERFACE; and it was the first to mix text and graphics indiscriminately on the screen. Yet despite all of these breakthroughs Macintosh languishes in a niche in computer markets. Ultimately Macintosh was brought low by the arrogance of its designers. Having designed an "insanely great" computer, Apple assumed first that people would pay a price premium for the machine, and second that they would instantly appreciate that the Macintosh way of doing things was the one true way. Neither was true, at least not to the extent that the Macintosh designers believed. By the time Apple learned humility, many of its distinctive features had been replicated by others, notably MICROSOFT'S WINDOWS.

If the automobile had followed the same development as the computer, a Rolls-Royce would today cost $100, get a million miles per gallon, and explode once a year killing everyone inside.
Robert X. Cringely

MACRO PROGRAMMING

Macros, as statements in macro-programming languages are called, are a simple form of programming which serve as a boon to those who hate to type. They come in two basic flavours. In an APPLICATION program (such as a SPREADSHEET), macros are a way of automating commonly performed sequences of operations. For example, an accountant reformatting a column of numbers time and again for a weekly report might wish to create an automated procedure to do the job with a single command. Some spreadsheets will help to write just such a macro by recording the usual sequence of key strokes to be stored as a new macro.

In programming languages macros achieve similar ends but by different means. Should programmers find themselves frequently repeating some long series of statements with a few variations, many languages allow them to write a macro which will enable them to type just the name of the macro, and from that recreate the whole set of statements. Because both sorts of macros hide what they are doing beneath a layer of convenience, they can make programs obscure and difficult for anybody other than the person who wrote the macro to work with. But they are useful.

MAILING LIST

Mailing lists take advantage of the ease with which E-MAIL can be duplicated to create privately organised discussion groups. E-mail sent to a central mailbox is automatically duplicated and sent to everyone on the list, which may contain thousands of names. Not surprisingly, mailing lists have sprung up across the INTERNET like mushrooms on an autumn morning – both private and open to all – to discuss just about anything and everything.

MAINFRAME

The kind of big computer that needs its own air-conditioned room and attendants to cater to its obscure whims. Mainframes are widely considered to be outdated dinosaurs, yet many corporations rely on them for the basic, and crucial, operations of accounting, payroll, and the like. The problem is that the machines were designed under very different assumptions about computer capabilities and economics than exist today.

Early mainframes cost $1m or so when that was a lot of money. The technology was young, cantankerous and unreliable. As it cost a large multiple of the annual salaries of those who would be employed to tend it, it made sense to throw a lot of time and people at managing the reliability and performance of the machine. Today, by contrast, a high-powered PERSONAL COMPUTER costs less than a month's salary for the programmers who make them work, and computing economics has been stood on its head.

The advantages and disadvantages of mainframes today are still largely determined by decisions made when the old economics still applied. Given proper management they can be rock-solid reliable. But they are expensive to buy and to run, at least as measured by cost per unit of computing horsepower, and developing new programs for them is relatively slow and cumbersome.

IBM introduced its first mainframe computer, the 701, in 1952.

MASTER
The copy from which other copies are made; usually, but not always, the original.

MASTER-SLAVE
Describes a relationship between two computers of the same sort as that applying to people of the same name. One tells the other what to do and when to do it – with no ifs, ands or buts. This is in contrast to a CLIENT-SERVER relationship, in which one machine is making requests of the other that may, in theory at least, be deferred.

MATERIALS REQUIREMENTS PLANNING
See MRP.

MATRIX
A name for CYBERSPACE coined by William Gibson in the novel *Neuromancer*. It is also a mathematical technique widely used in computer graphics and neural nets, where several different equations must be applied simultaneously.

MATRIX PRINTER
A type of computer PRINTER which forms characters using a rectangular matrix of fine needles. To form, for example, the letter a, the print-head strikes the ribbon with only those needles which will form the shape of the letter. Although matrix printers are getting better, the marks of individual needles can still typically be seen in the resulting image which gives it a dotty, computerish look.

M

MEETING SUPPORT SYSTEMS

SOFTWARE and other tools designed to enable a group of people to work together more productively. In theory, at least, computers can help people both to share information and to reach consensus. But taking advantage of these abilities can be tricky.

Experience has shown that people will speak more freely over E-MAIL than face to face. So electronic discussions are useful for overcoming social barriers that might otherwise hinder brainstorming. Similarly, computers can provide everybody in a meeting with a record of what has been said, or reach into remote databases for relevant facts.

Often the hardest part of using computers productively in a meeting, however, is to shift from sharing information to building consensus. Computers can be used for anonymous voting on issues of interest. But it is often hard to create electronically the emotional commitment from which true consensus is built. So many meeting-support systems employ a trained facilitator to work alongside the machines, thus leaving information to the machines and emotions to the humans.

MEGA-

Strictly, a prefix denoting 1 million, but as the computer world counts in twos instead of tens, it here means 1,048,576 (the nearest power of two).

MEMORY

Where DATA and programs are stored on a computer. Computer memory comes in two basic forms. Main memory sits inside the machine, and holds data on SEMICONDUCTOR memory chips. Computers that run a variety of different programs use RAM, or, more specifically, DRAM. Appliances and computer games, which simply repeat the same programs over and over again, use ROM. Retrieval from main memory is quick, in the order of a few billionths of a second. But main memory is relatively expensive and often impermanent. Any information stored in RAM disappears when the power is turned off.

Secondary memory includes disks, tape and other more permanent media. These are slower: the fastest serve up data within thousandths of a second and some take even longer. But they are cheap and they store data for years, even with the power switched off. At least most of the time they store data for years (see also CRASH and BACK-UP).

MENU
Key component of a MENU-DRIVEN INTERFACE.

MENU-DRIVEN INTERFACE
A computer INTERFACE which allows users to choose commands from a menu of alternatives that pops up on the screen. This is an easier-to-use but less flexible alternative to a COMMAND-LINE INTERFACE, which requires users to type commands on to a blank screen (and thus also requires them to remember what all the commands are).

METHODOLOGY
A discipline for designing and building computer systems. The heart of a methodology is a way of analysing business systems, and representing that analysis in a form that can, in turn, be turned into working computer programs. The hope is that a disciplined approach will yield better results.

There is no shortage of methodologies to choose from. Nearly all IT departments and consultants have their own, each with advantages and disadvantages. But all methodologies suffer from a generic limitation. As IT projects become larger, even well-constructed systems increasingly risk being irrelevant by the time they are completed. Discipline takes time, and the underlying business and its markets will seldom sit still for an IT project that stretches over four or five years.

More importantly, the disciplines of most methodologies require people to predict at the start how they will use their computers four or five years hence. Few can imagine just how radically computers can change their lives and the way they do business. So the discipline of methodologies has a nasty habit of locking companies into the status quo. For this reason, many companies are turning from the WATERFALL MODEL of systems development assumed by most methodologies to a SPIRAL MODEL, which is based on rapidly building a prototype of a new system and then steadily improving upon it.

MICROCOMPUTER

Another name for a personal computer. A computer powered by its own MICROPROCESSOR which, unlike a minicomputer, is typically designed to serve only one person at a time.

The MITS Altair, launched in 1975, was the first microcomputer. It cost $350 and had to be soldered together by its proud owner.

MICROPROCESSOR

A CPU which has been constructed on a single piece of silicon. Elements of a microprocessor include the following.

- **ALU** (arithmetic logic unit), which does basic calculations.
- **FPU** (floating-point unit), which does more advanced calculations involving FLOATING-POINT ARITHMETIC.
- **CACHE**, which is a local BUFFER to hold MACHINE CODE soon to be executed and DATA soon to be worked on, for faster access than can be achieved from MEMORY.
- **REGISTER**, which is a kind of electronic workbench to hold the data being operated on by current instructions.

Bill Gates dropped out of Harvard in 1975 to write a version of the BASIC programming language for the MITS Altair after seeing it featured on the cover of Popular Electronics. Thus Microsoft was born.

MICROSOFT

Founded by a teenage programming whiz-kid, Bill

M

Gates, in 1976, Microsoft had by the 1990s become the most powerful company in the computer world. Microsoft owes its strength to its dominance in the field of operating systems for personal computers, and it owes that, in turn, to IBM.

In 1980 Bill Gates made his living selling a version of the BASIC programming language for personal computers. IBM was rushing to create a PERSONAL COMPUTER to compete with APPLE when it approached Mr Gates to licence his programming languages. Almost as an afterthought, it also asked him for an OPERATING SYSTEM. He quickly bought the rights to a basic operating system from Seattle Computer Products, a nearby firm, improved it and renamed it DOS. Thus an empire was born.

A deeply determined businessman, Mr Gates steadily added a variety of other products to his range: WORD PROCESSOR, SPREADSHEET, other programming languages, and so on. Microsoft's hallmark was determination. Some of its products were not well received on their first release, or even their second. But in any product category which he deemed strategically important, Mr Gates simply kept trying until he got it right. To its credit, Microsoft usually did get it right in the end, and both its word processing and its spreadsheet SOFTWARE wrested dominance of their market sectors from established competitors.

Probably the most important of Microsoft's long-term bets was WINDOWS, a program which provides an easy-to-use GUI for IBM-COMPATIBLE computers. The first two releases of Windows went nowhere, but the third took off like a skyrocket. Windows now sells millions of copies each month, and gives Microsoft the key to its market power: control of the INTERFACE between man and computer, and between application programs (like word processors) and the underlying computer.

Microsoft is now trying to adapt Windows for all sorts of other computing devices, including smart cellular telephones, MULTI-TASKING computers and the set-top box which controls cable television. The USA's trustbusters, meanwhile, have spent years investigating allegations that Microsoft unfairly used its dominance in operating systems to help its applications software succeed against competitors. Meanwhile, Mr Gates has seen his personal fortune soar to over $7 billion.

MICROWAVE
A high-FREQUENCY electromagnetic signal often used for communications.

MIDI
Short for Musical Instrument Digital Interface, a STANDARD for exchanging DATA between a computer and a music synthesiser.

MILNET
The portion of the INTERNET used and financed by the US military.

MIMD
Short for Multiple Instructions, Multiple Data, a form of PARALLEL PROCESSING in which each processor can execute a different instruction on different DATA. This is in contrast to SIMD (Single Instruction, Multiple Data), where each processor executes the same instruction at the same time. SIMD is like a row of reapers, swishing their scythes in unison as they move across a field of wheat. MIMD is more like the division of labour within a mill, where one person bags ground flour while another turns the mill-stone, while yet another prepares grain. As you would expect, each approach is suited to different problems.

MIME
Abbreviation for Multipurpose Internet Mailing Extensions, a way of sending MULTIMEDIA – sound, pictures, formatted text or whatever – over the INTERNET via SMTP mailing protocols, which were originally designed to handle only ASCII text.

MINICOMPUTER
An intermediate-sized computer, typically capable of serving tens of users rather than the hundreds

that a MAINFRAME serves and the one served by a PERSONAL COMPUTER. In the 1970s minicomputers were the hottest thing around because they made it possible to apply computers to tasks otherwise too small to automate. By the early 1990s, however, markets for minicomputers were vanishing following the advent of CLIENT-SERVER computing. In effect, client-server split the work of the mini-computer in two. Tasks done directly for users, like word processing, had been handed over to near-ubiquitous personal computers. Meanwhile, databases – and other information-sharing and management tasks – were being performed by specialised FILE SERVER and NETWORK machines, often a UNIX WORKSTATION.

Benjamin Curley created the first minicomputer in 1960 at Digital Equipment Corporation.

MIPS

Millions of Instructions Per Second, a commonly used measure of the speed of a computer. MIPS is the number of assembly-language statements that a given machine executes in an average second. The problem with MIPS, however, is that all instructions are not alike. Some chips do a lot more work with each instruction than others, so simple counts of instructions executed do not necessarily reflect accurately the amount of computing work done.

One way around this problem is to try statistically to compensate by creating an artificial, standardised instruction that reflects differences in the amount of work. So-called VAX MIPS, based on the performance of DEC'S VAX computers, are often used for this purpose. Another way round the problem would be to use an alternative measure of performance. But computer-makers cannot agree on what the fairest and generally best alternative might be. (The best way to measure performance is simply to put your favourite program on the machine and see how quickly it goes for you.)

M

MNP-4
An error-correction PROTOCOL for a MODEM.

MNP-5
The same as MNP-4, but it also compresses DATA.

MODEM
Acronym for Modulator-Demodulator, a device that translates a stream of DIGITAL DATA into a staccato series of bleeps and bloops that can be sent over a telephone line, or some other ANALOGUE communications channel. More specifically, it is a device that does, and undoes, MODULATION.

MODERATED
Describes a NEWS GROUP or MAILING LIST in which the flow of contributions is controlled by an editor, or moderator. Instead of simply passing along all messages, as most news groups do, the moderator tries to cut the flow of information down to manageable size by weeding out those judged unworthy of a general readership.

MODULARITY
In reference to SOFTWARE, modularity describes the extent to which a program can be broken down into discrete, independently functioning components. One of the lessons that programmers learned the hard way is that it is very easy to construct programs in which everything effectively depends on everything else, and very hard to live with them. Any change or modification in the SPAGHETTI CODE of a program with insufficient modularity can cause a breakdown in a seemingly unrelated part of the program. In the 1970s, however, disciplines of so-called STRUCTURED PROGRAMMING were created to help programmers to divide programs into smaller and more manageable component modules.

MODULATION
The act of encoding information into a CARRIER wave by altering its AMPLITUDE, PHASE, or FREQUENCY. Normally the carrier wave is of constant ampli-

tude, frequency and phase. By changing one or
more of these attributes in predetermined ways, a
MODEM can use modulation to send information
across a communications channel.

MODULO

A mathematical operation related to division,
except that instead of returning the dividend it
returns the remainder. Thus 14 divided by 4 is 3,
but 14 modulo 4 is 2.

MONITOR

A computer screen. (See COMPOSITE MONITOR and
RGB MONITOR.)

MOO

Short for MUD OBJECT ORIENTED. A MOO is a MUD
(multi-user dungeon) with a programming language built in, so that, instead of just wandering
around an imaginary world inside the machine, its
users can shape the world to their own whims. A
MOO is a kind of consensual hallucination, the
nearest computer scientists have yet managed to
approach the vision of the MATRIX created by the
science fiction writer, William Gibson.

So far MOOS are mostly for fun. The Cyberion
City MOO, hosted by a computer at MIT, allows its
users to create a world within a future space sta-
tion. Other MOOS involve magic and sorcery; others still are populated by people who like to
fantasise that they are small furry animals which,
untrue to character, seem to spend a lot of time in
a hot tub talking about their feelings.

The programming language built into MOOS
gives their users great freedom to shape both their
characters and the world around them. In a MUD,
both the objects in the world and the actions that
can be performed with them are created in
advance, by the original programmers. In a MOO,
users can create their own objects and actions. If
someone is dissatisfied with the fire-breathing
dragons supplied by the original programmers,
they can create dragons with curry-breath, fire-
breathing mice, or whatever.

The result of this freedom has been an outpouring of both creativity and just plain messing around. People can create their own characters in a MOO, and many use the opportunity to try out a new personality. Some become flamboyant; some change sex; and some just try to create things and experiences that they could not have in the real world. Given the creativity that MOOs can unleash, researchers hope to adapt the basic technology for education and to help geographically remote workers create virtual open-plan offices in which they can collaborate as if they worked shoulder to shoulder.

MOSAIC
See WEB BROWSER.

MOTHERBOARD
A computer's central circuit board, into which plug the MICROPROCESSOR, MEMORY and other essential components of the machine. The motherboard provides the BUS which links together all of the computer's components, and is not to be confused with peripherals, enhancements or plug-in cards.

MOTIF
Extensions to the X WINDOWS system used on many UNIX WORKSTATIONS. Motif was designed to make X better-looking and easier to use than the basic X system. Some say it succeeds.

MOUSE
The most popular form of pointing device for computers. Mice have a button or buttons on top and some kind of motion detector on the bottom. Move the mouse across the desktop and it moves an on-screen pointer, or CURSOR. Click a button and it selects the screen object underneath the cursor, to do whatever operation is appropriate in the given program at the given time (which is also, hopefully but not necessarily, what the mouse-pusher intended).

The mouse was invented by Douglas Engelbart

at the Stanford Research Institute in the early 1970s, adopted by his neighbours just down the road at Xerox's Palo Alto Research Center and popularised by APPLE's MACINTOSH computer. For such humble devices, mice have sparked a surprising amount of discussion. Early mice had two buttons. Steve Jobs, who led the design of the Macintosh, insisted that its mouse have only one button, lest its users be overwhelmed by the difficulties of telling left from right. Most mice on a UNIX WORKSTATION, by contrast, have three buttons, because the nerds who run them insist on more choices (and if you can master Unix, three buttons on a mouse is simplicity itself).

MOVING PICTURES EXPERTS GROUP
See MPEG below.

MPEG
For Moving Pictures Experts Group. Standards which compress video and other moving pictures into a size that can be more easily stored on a CD-ROM or transmitted across a network. The grail of MPEG is so-called full-screen, full-motion video – which, as the name implies, would include every frame of motion at a size to cover a full screen.

MRP
Short for Materials Requirement Planning, a system commonly used to automate production scheduling, including ordering the appropriate raw materials.

MUD
Abbreviation for Multi-User Dungeon, a computerised version of fantasy role-playing games. Players take on a character, traditionally from the swords-and-sorcery selection of trolls, magicians, knights, and so on. Then they LOG ON to a central computer, where, by typing commands like north (to go north) or fight (to attack another character) they can wander blissfully through an imaginary world. MUDS were created at the University of Essex in the UK, but MUDS and MOOS, their more

advanced relations, have since become one of the leading causes of computer addiction at campuses across the world.

For some people playing a character in a fantasy world can quickly become more interesting and compelling than classes, personal hygiene, or sleep. Campus folklore is now full of stories of promising students who sacrificed career and sanity for a chance of reaching wizard level (the highest) in the character of, say, Rotifer the Mag. Some university administrators have become so concerned about the amount of time students spend playing in a MUD that they have banned them from campus machines. Meanwhile, researchers elsewhere reckon that any technology which can so powerfully grip the human imagination must have some useful potential in it somewhere. So they are trying to use the principles of MUDs to design virtual worlds for collaboration among far-flung researchers (for more discussion of which see MOO).

MULTICAST

A form of broadcasting, adapted for efficiency on computer networks like the INTERNET. The problem with broadcasting over networks is that it wastes communications capacity. The obvious way of sending the same message to thousands of people is simply to send each a copy. But that means that many, perhaps thousands or millions, of copies of the same communication will clog the central backbone of the NETWORK, travelling one after the other. Multicasting tries to eliminate this inefficiency. The trick is to postpone the act of copying until the last possible moment, when communications routes to different destinations diverge. So, for example, if ten recipients are on the same LOCAL AREA NETWORK, then multicasting will send only one copy of the message to the GATEWAY that links the local area network to the Internet. Copies will be created only on the local network, which greatly eases congestion. Experiments in multicasting have included attempts to deliver radio-style talk shows over the Internet.

MULTIMEDIA

Just what the word says: multimedia is the combination of different media – text, video, audio,
graphics, and so on – with a bit of computing
power to hold them all together. To deliver multimedia requires a high-BANDWIDTH communications
channel, either NETWORK or CD-ROM. The hope, and
hype, is that by combining different media,
"authors" (or however multimediators are
described) will be able to create things new and
more wonderfully informative and educational
than any yet dreamed of. The risk, of course, is
that they will instead create a noisy, flashy mess.
While the promise is bright, actual performance is
so far finely balanced.

*The medium is the message. This is just to say that
the personal and social consequences of any
medium – that is, of any extension of ourselves –
result from the new scale that is introduced into
our affairs ...*
Marshall McLuhan

MULTIPLEX

To combine several signals for transmission over
the same communications channel. One of the
most common forms of multiplexing is TIME DIVI-
SION MULTIPLEXING, in which the channel is divided
up by time slots. Each signal has its own series of
very short time slots. From millisecond to millisecond, the multiplexor interleaves each signal's time
slots with the others. Another commonly used form
of multiplexing is FREQUENCY division multiplexing,
in which each signal is assigned its own band of
frequencies within the channel. The obvious point
of multiplexing is to use channel capacity to maximum efficiency. Yet another form of multiplexing
is code division multiple access or CDMA.

MULTI-PROCESSOR

Describes computers which share work among
more than one MICROPROCESSOR. A modern FILE
SERVER, for example, may use as many as half a

dozen microprocessors. When there are many requests pending, it allocates tasks among microprocessors for fast service. When there are only a few, it gives each microprocessor a part of the task. This provides a cheap and flexible way of bringing maximum processing power to bear on a task.

MULTIPURPOSE INTERNET MAILING EXTENSIONS
See MIME.

MULTI-TASKING
Describes computers which execute several programs at once. Historically, the impetus for multi-tasking came from the observation that input and output typically took several orders of magnitude longer than any calculating the machine might do. Thus a typical program kept the CPU, the most expensive part of the computer, waiting for the vast majority of the time it occupied the machine. So some bright spark came up with the fairly obvious idea of sharing the CPU, letting programs with calculations ready to go use the CPU while others wait for input or output. When all goes well the result is a machine which appears to be at the personal command of several different people at once. When the machine gets overloaded – by too many people or too many calculation-intensive tasks – the result is annoying delays.

MUSICAL INSTRUMENT DIGITAL INTERFACE
See MIDI.

NACK
Negative Acknowledgement, which symbolises a code commonly used in communications protocols to denote that the message has been garbled or in some way messed up (contrast to ACK).

NAME SERVER
A computer on a NETWORK which translates mnemonic machine names and addresses – which people use to, for example, address E-MAIL – into the sequences of numbers which machines use to talk to other machines.

NATIONAL TELEVISION STANDARDS COMMITTEE
See NTSC.

NERD
Someone whose enthusiasm for playing with technology overshadows that for many other aspects of life, like socialising or washing. The archetypal nerd is male and dresses largely in polyester and plaid. His glasses are held together with a safety pin and spotted with dandruff. His pockets are full of felt-tip pens, calculators, paper clips and a small-office-worth of useful stuff. His wristwatch has more functions than most computers. While nerds may not have had the most dates at school, many now have earnings that make their ex-classmates blush. As *California* magazine asked when it put a nerd on its cover at the height of the PERSONAL COMPUTER boom in the mid-1980s: "Who's laughing now?"

> *Anyone who spends their life on a computer is pretty unusual.*
> Bill Gates

NETIQUETTE
NETWORK manners. Like all human societies, computer networks have developed their own codes of conduct. Netiquette is a combination of the basic technical knowledge needed to avoid making a nuisance of yourself – like understanding

how to use a knife and fork at the table – with common sense and respect for others.

NETSCAPE

The most popular SOFTWARE used to view the global NETWORK of hypermedia that makes up the WORLD WIDE WEB. It became the most popular in part because the company that makes Netscape gave the software away in the hope of building up a base of users to which it could sell other, more advanced services.

NETWORK

A collection of things or people linked together to share INFORMATION. Examples include the telephone network, the INTERNET, the Old Boy network, and so on.

NETWORK LAYER

That part of the SEVEN LAYER REFERENCE MODEL which concerns technologies for routing a PACKET between one machine and another across a NETWORK.

NEURAL NET

A way of computing that is based on the wiring of the brain rather than the symbolic reasoning of the mind. Neural nets are composed of many small processors connected together. These connections are the key to the workings of a neural net. The computing done by each processor node is quite simple. Each node either sends a signal or remains silent. That decision, in turn is based on the signals sent to the node. If the strength of the incoming signals is greater than some threshold value, the node sends its own signal to all of the nodes to which it is connected.

Neural nets are taught to recognise complex patterns by adjusting the strength of the signals between nodes, hence the effect that each node has on the others to which it is connected. Signals can either inhibit the firing of a node or promote it, and each signal can be given a weight, which determines how strongly it will inhibit or promote.

Much of the recent enthusiasm for neural models of computation stems from the discovery of techniques for adjusting the weights on signals which can reliably enable the net to associate inputs with outputs, that is, to recognise patterns.

Neural nets are now being used to recognise handwriting, to search for patterns in stock-price movements and to recognise the road (and so help to build a car that can drive itself). The advantages of neural nets are twofold. They can recognise patterns far more complex than can be managed by conventional computers – faces, for example – and, because they use so many processors in parallel, they can do so quickly. Better still, the performance of neural nets degrades gracefully. They do not stop working all at once but instead, like people, simply make more and more errors as they encounter increasingly unfamiliar patterns.

Against these advantages, however, must be weighed the time and care that must be taken in training the nets: in successively showing them examples of right answers and wrong ones, and adjusting the connections between nodes to enable the net to distinguish one from the other. Another drawback of neural nets is their inability to explain how they have reached their conclusion. Because computation is quite literally spread across all of the processors that make up a net, there is no central consciousness which can explain to a sceptical observer how the net reached a given conclusion. This means that, in practice, using a neural net is quite literally an act of faith.

According to the market researchers at Inteco, 17% of European households had personal computers in 1994, versus 37% in the United States. Only 1.6% of Europeans used computer bulletin boards or other on-line services, compared with 14% in the United States.

NEWS GROUP
An electronic forum for the discussion of a given topic. About 12,000 news groups now make up

the USENET, a part of the INTERNET devoted to debate on topics ranging from sex to high-energy physics. News groups are open to all, and are organised as an exchange of E-MAIL messages.

NEWS READER
A program used to read USENET news. News readers help to organise E-MAIL into a discussion of a specific subject. Mail is sorted by subject and time, so that someone entering the group discussion can follow the thread of electronic argument between many participants. Responses, in turn, are automatically sent to the proper address, with the proper subject.

NNTP
Short for Net News Transfer Protocol, the most commonly used PROTOCOL for transferring USENET news groups between one machine and another.

NOISE
Something which disrupts the flow of INFORMATION across a communications channel. The noisier a channel, the less information it can carry. The phrase "noise-to-signal ratio" refers to the relative quantities of each.

NOR
A logical operation performed in SOFTWARE or in circuitry. It returns true (or on) if and only if both inputs are false (or off); otherwise it returns false.

NOVELL
The name of both the leading technology for creating a LOCAL AREA NETWORK with an IBM-COMPATIBLE computer and the company that makes it.

NSFNET
The portion of the INTERNET funded by the USA's National Science Foundation (NSF). For many years the NSFNET was the backbone of the Internet, a crucial long-haul service to move data from one side of the world to the other. However, as the Internet has matured the government has reduced

funding for the NSFNET, asking users to switch to commercial services.

NTSC

For National Television Standards Committee. Used to describe the technical standard for television transmissions in most of the Americas – although strictly, of course, the standard should be NTS, set by the NTSC. It makes up a picture of 525 lines of dots. (Contrast to PAL and SECAM.)

OBJECT DATABASE

An OBJECT-ORIENTED approach to storing DATA in a DATABASE. In addition to storing the data itself, object-oriented databases store INFORMATION about what can sensibly be done with the data. In effect, the object-oriented database tries to keep its data in context. It knows that a drawing from a COMPUTER AIDED DESIGN program is entirely different from last year's financial results, even if all the computer itself can see in both cases is a bunch of BITS.

OBJECT LINKING AND EMBEDDING

See OLE.

OBJECT ORIENTED

Describes an approach to programming first popularised in the 1980s with the language Smalltalk, which attempts to build programs out of SOFTWARE objects whose capabilities mirror those of the real world. For example, a "bank account" object, would store within itself its own balance, and it would know how to respond to messages making requests like "withdraw £50" or "deposit £1,000".

Three key ideas underlie this programming approach.

- Inheritance is a convenient way of capturing the similarities between things. All bank accounts share basic features in common. They have a balance, for example, and they must cope with money coming in and going out. Yet accounts also differ in other ways: how they calculate interest, or whether they offer an overdraft. Inheritance offers a way of sharing the common parts of an object, while still providing freedom for each object to add more specialised capabilities of its own. It saves time and money in large software projects. With inheritance, the common capabilities of a group of objects – like querying an account balance, for example – need be written only once; more specialised objects can then "inherit" that code. With inheritance, a designer can also enforce disciplines on the interface which objects present to the world; for example, by requiring that all "bank account" objects should at least be capable of taking a deposit or accepting a withdrawal, but without specifying exactly how they should do so.

- Polymorphism captures the idea that related objects might wish to do conceptually similar things in different ways. A cheque account with overdraft, for example, will deal with withdrawals differently from one without. In order to make polymorphism work in practice, it is crucial that no object should make assumptions about how another object does its work, apart from the necessary belief that, given a request and the necessary input, it will return a sensible answer. This in turn makes objects easier to modify, improve and change.

- Messages are the way in which things get done in an object-oriented world. Traditional programming languages talk about actions in terms of imperatives, that is, starting from the verb. So they would say something like "withdraw £50 from account X". But this approach sits uneasily with polymorphism because it leaves on the programmer's shoulders the responsibility for determining which of the many ways of making a withdrawal is appropriate for account X, and programmers often get it wrong. So object-oriented approaches put the noun in front of the verb to make the context clear. Instead of simply ordering an action, they send a message making a request: "Please, account X, do whatever it is you do when you make a withdrawal, in the amount of £50."

While Smalltalk is still the purists' favourite object-oriented programming language, its popularity is being eclipsed by c++, a language that fits more easily into the environment in which object-oriented approaches thrive: the networked world of CLIENT-SERVER computing. The idea of sending messages to objects fits neatly into the world of distributed computing, where instead of withdrawing from a bank account, a program might send a message asking "please, PRINTER, print this with the highest quality you can manage". Given emerging standards like CORBA to help objects locate other objects with the capabilities they need, and negotiate to use them, object-oriented approaches could make even the biggest and most complex networks much more manageable.

OFF LINE

Lacking a NETWORK connection to another computer. In practice, it is a phrase most often used by a NERD as a synonym for "after the meeting", as in, "let's discuss that off-line, after I've finished my presentation".

OLE

Object Linking and Embedding, a STANDARD proposed by MICROSOFT which tries to apply object-oriented technology to make it easier for computer programs to work together. If, for example, a chart from a SPREADSHEET is embedded in a document being word-processed, the standard helps the various SOFTWARE involved to know how and when to update the chart to reflect changes in the underlying spreadsheet. (See also OPENDOC.)

ON LINE

The opposite of OFF LINE; that is, enjoying a NETWORK connection to another computer.

CompuServe and The Source became the first on-line information sources in 1979.

OPEN SYSTEM

One of the most abused phrases in information technology. Open system describes technology which is accessible for everybody to use, but as no one in their right mind would want to make their product inaccessible, everyone finds some way to shoe-horn their product into some definition of open system. So the word should be treated with some suspicion.

The most truly open system is probably UNIX (some people use open system as a synonym for Unix). Unix was developed by AT&T's Bell Labs while AT&T was still the USA's regulated telephone monopoly, and thus forbidden from commercially exploiting computer innovations. So the source code for Unix was freely distributed for all to explore and copy. For most open systems only a description of the INTERFACE – that is, the way in which the system interacts with other SOFTWARE and HARDWARE – is made publicly available. The completeness of that description determines how much hyperbole lies in its claims for openness.

OPENDOC

A technical STANDARD proposed by IBM, APPLE and others to make it easier for various pieces of SOFTWARE to work together. If, say, a chart from a SPREADSHEET is embedded in a document from a WORD PROCESSOR, the standard enables the various software involved to know how and when to update the chart to reflect changes in the underlying spreadsheet. (See also OLE.)

OPERATING SYSTEM

A key part of the infrastructure of computing, operating systems provide the basic capabilities from which applications can be built. In practice, this means hiding from applications SOFTWARE like word processors and spreadsheets many of the complexities of the machines they are working on. Among other things, operating systems typically manage the following.

- **MULTI-TASKING.** When programs share a CPU, the operating system is responsible for managing which program gets to run when.
- **Input and output.** Operating systems manage printers, tape drives and other input and output devices. Apart from administering the process of input and output – preventing pro-

grams from interfering with each other and monitoring whether printers and so on are working or not – they also provide a simplified INTERFACE which hides from the program the complexities of the HARDWARE of any input or output device. This makes it easier to swap around peripherals as new models become available.

- **Files.** Managing the reading and writing of DATA to DISK is a form of input and output that takes up a huge proportion of the time and effort put into operating systems.

- MEMORY. The operating system loads programs into memory and ensures that they neither overlap nor interfere with each other's allocations of memory. Through techniques known as VIRTUAL MEMORY, some operating systems can run programs which are larger than the actual amount of memory in the machine. The trick is to swap parts of the program to and from disk as needed.

- **Networks.** Operating systems provide an interface to networks which, like other input and output interfaces, hides from applications programs much of the complexity of the underlying NETWORK.

- SECURITY. Operating systems enforce the security measures necessary to keep sensitive data secret, and to prevent even malicious users from messing up the work of their colleagues.

- SYSTEMS ADMINISTRATION. Perhaps the least interesting, but most important, features of any operating system are the collection of tools provided for the housekeeping chores necessary to manage any computer system: to back up data, to monitor and adjust performance and to allocate scarce resources like disk space.

OPERATIONS RESEARCH

Describes a set of techniques and disciplines aimed at making managerial decision-making more scientific. Operations research includes much of LINEAR PROGRAMMING, statistical reasoning and other mathematical techniques aimed at finding optimal solutions to complex problems, where knowledge may be uncertain.

OPTICAL DISK

A DISK in which DATA are read and written with a laser. The trick lies in finding materials that can be made reflective or not, repeatedly, quickly and easily. Early optical disks simply burnt away a reflective coating with a laser, making them into WORM disks, which could be written only once. With modern materials to create disks that can be written and rewritten repeatedly, the optical disk is gradually taking over from the TAPE DRIVE for storage of large quantities of data.

OR

An operation or circuit which returns true (or on) if one or more of its inputs is true (or on).

OS/2

IBM's next-generation OPERATING SYSTEM for the PERSONAL COMPUTER. OS/2 is personal computing's great might-have-been. It is a MULTI-TASKING operating system with a graphical INTERFACE which is by most accounts technically excellent. Yet it has received only lukewarm acceptance in the marketplace, thanks in large part to a damaging split between IBM and MICROSOFT.

Originally developed in a partnership between IBM and Microsoft, it seemed certain to dominate the market. Then, around 1990, IBM and Microsoft began to drift apart. Microsoft said its customers really wanted WINDOWS, a less capable operating system which did not require as much computing horse-power to run. IBM, meanwhile, imposed a development bureaucracy on OS/2 which was alien to Microsoft's HACKER culture. By the time the two had split Microsoft had grabbed the momentum in the marketplace with strong sales of Windows which, unlike OS/2, was already shipping. Now Microsoft is trying to push customers to upgrade Windows to new multi-tasking versions

O

like Windows NT, while IBM is trying to catch up with Windows's marketing momentum.

IBM: Fast, Accurate, Stupid
Man: Slow, Sloppy, Smart
Sign in IBM's Tokyo office

PABX

Short for Private Automatic Branch Exchange, a privately owned and operated telephone switch which serves as the switchboard for a typical office. PABXs typically handle tens or hundreds of lines, and, unlike old-fashioned switchboards, they do so without requiring banks of operators manually to plug one line into another.

PACKET

A way of organising DATA for communication. Instead of a steady stream of BITS and BYTES, most computer communications split data into discrete packets. As well as data, each packet typically contains the address to which the packet is being sent, a number which denotes that packet's place in the sequence, and information which helps to detect and correct errors. Some packets also contain information about what type of data is being sent. Others serve administrative functions in setting up routes and managing the flow of data.

The advantage of packets is their flexibility and efficiency. Packets from different communications can easily be intermixed to maximise use of a line. Packets from the same communication can travel by different routes to speed passage over a crowded network. Given the speed of today's computers, packets can easily carry time-sensitive data, like interactive video, or voice conversations. But the drawback to packet data is, nonetheless, the extra overhead of splitting data into packets at one end and recombining them at the other.

PACKET-SWITCHED

Describes a NETWORK that sends DATA one PACKET at a time, and so does not keep open a connection between two machines when no data is flowing between them. For many applications, particularly with computer data, the extra overheads of addressing each packet separately are well worth the savings in efficiency gained from not holding open temporarily unused connections. (Contrast to CIRCUIT-SWITCHED.)

PAGING

A way of managing VIRTUAL MEMORY, in which standard sized chunks of program and/or DATA are swapped into MEMORY when needed and temporarily stashed back on DISK when not. Because paging is a relatively slow operation and does not contribute directly to the progress of computation, how a computer manages paging is a key issue in its overall performance. Paging is also a system for mobile communications whereby a simple message is sent to a pocket terminal.

PAL

Short for Phase Alteration by Line, a colour television STANDARD developed in the UK and used there and in Germany. It makes up a picture with 625 lines of dots. (Contrast to NTSC and SECAM.)

PARALLEL COMMUNICATIONS

Describes a form of communications in which several BITS are sent simultaneously, in contrast to SERIAL communications in which they are sent one after the other. The extra speed of parallel communications has made it popular for sending DATA to printers, but the fine timing required to make sure that all the bits arrive at the same time limits its use to relatively short distances. Hence also parallel port, the connection where the wires for parallel communications are plugged in.

PARALLEL PROCESSING

Attacking the same problem with several processors at once. Like the proverb, the assumption behind parallel processing is that "many hands make light work".

A rough and ready classification of parallel processing would divide into three categories.

- **Multiprocessing.** Many file servers, for example, share their work among half a dozen or so processors. When one is overloaded, another lends a helping hand.
- **Parallel supercomputers.** Machines from N-Cube, INTEL and a variety of other com-

panies aim for high-speed computation by putting tens or hundreds of processors to work on the same problem. Such machines are used to forecast the weather, analyse stress on aircraft wings and search vast databases quickly. The processors can work either in strict synchronisation (see SIMD) or with a looser co-ordination in which the problem is split into several chunks, and each processor tackles its chunks at its own speed (see MIMD).

- **Neural nets.** A NEURAL NET contains hundreds or even thousands of simple processors. While the capabilities of each individual processor are limited, the connections between them enable neural nets to recognise complex patterns.

While parallel processing can indeed improve results on many problems, researchers face two challenges in taking advantage of its full potential. The first is simply the intellectual sweat of recasting the solutions to problems in a form that allows different parts of the work to be done simultaneously. Second, and hardest, those solutions must ensure that the time spent co-ordinating results among different processors does not overwhelm the extra speed gained from having more "brains" at work. Some people feel that such co-ordination problems will place the ultimate limits on the extra speed to be gained from parallelisation. Others are hard at work trying to crack those limits.

In 1958 the Harvard Business Review *predicted that the economy of the 1980s would be dominated by a handful of giant corporations, each organised around a single huge computer.*

PARITY
Describes a scheme for detecting and correcting errors in which each piece of DATA is required to have an even or odd number of BITS. If the num-

ber naturally comes out the wrong way, an extra BIT, called the parity bit, is turned on to make it right. This scheme should detect all one-bit errors, or indeed all errors involving an odd number of bits. But it is not much good for two-bit errors. Nevertheless, its speed and ease of use has made it popular for monitoring computer MEMORY.

PASCAL

A programming language created by a Swiss computer scientist, Niklaus Wirth. For most of the 1980s it was the first language taught to young computer scientists, and it has been highly influential in shaping ideas about STRUCTURED PROGRAMMING and the proper style of a program. The simplicity that makes it excellent for teaching, however, has limited its use in real, workaday programming.

PASSWORD

A sequence of characters which serves as a kind of text key in gaining access to computers. To maintain SECURITY, passwords should be known only to their owners and be hard to guess. The perennial dilemma in managing passwords, however, is that hard-to-guess passwords – that is, words which are not in the dictionary and which contain numbers and/or punctuation marks – are also hard to remember.

PATCH

A correction or improvement to a program that is distributed as a snippet of code, together with instructions on how and where the new code is to be stitched into the old program.

PC

See PERSONAL COMPUTER.

PC-COMPATIBLE

See IBM-COMPATIBLE.

PCI

Short for Peripheral Components Interface, a fast

P

computer BUS, quick enough for both video and graphics, which is now becoming standard on IBM-COMPATIBLE computers.

PCMCIA

Abbreviation for Personal Computer Memory Card International Association, a series of technical standards for the creation of small (as small as credit-card sized) circuit boards that can be plugged into personal computers to add a MODEM, networking capabilities or other enhancements.

PCN

See PERSONAL COMMUNICATIONS NETWORK.

PDA

Short for Personal Digital Assistant, a new form of computer which is meant to fit into a jacket pocket (well, given a very large jacket) and travel everywhere with its owner. Progenitor of the breed was APPLE's Newton, a machine designed to do several useful things at once, including the following.

- **Communications.** Using either a wireless MODEM or a plug into the telephone network, PDAS can send and receive faxes, E-MAIL and DATA.
- **Diary.** PDAS typically come equipped with SOFTWARE to manage appointments and to keep track of addresses and other personal information.
- **Notes.** PDAS are also typically designed to take and store notes, and to write simple memos and letters.

So far so useful. But the snag with PDAS is getting information into the machines in the first place. Designers of the original PDAS assumed that technology for handwriting recognition – that is, for a computer automatically and accurately to convert human scrawl into ASCII characters – would make PDAS the first of a new breed of pen-based computers. But the inaccuracy of handwriting technology made early PDAS a joke instead of a success. Unfortunately, any keyboard small enough to fit into a jacket pocket is also too small to use comfortably.

PEN-BASED COMPUTING
Computers that take their input from a pen-like stylus rather than a keyboard. Characters and text-based DATA would be input through handwriting recognition, whereby the computer translated human scrawl into ASCII characters. Graphics and free-hand drawings could be stored using DIGITAL ink; that is, by simply recording the path of the stylus over the screen as a sequence of BITS and BYTES. Commands to the computer would often come in the form of gestures, like ticks (to choose from a MENU) or the proof-reader's deletion mark (to delete text).

Unfortunately the general inadequacy of early handwriting recognition programs meant that pen-based computers failed to live up to their early hype. Instead of replacing the keyboard, pen-based machines were more or less restricted to applications where a keyboard could not be used. They have nonetheless proved extremely useful in helping mobile workers, like warehouse staff and insurance claims adjusters, to automate many of the forms they fill in.

PERIPHERAL
A device which attaches to a computer; for example, a PRINTER, TAPE DRIVE, PLOTTER, external DISK drive, or the like.

PERSONAL COMMUNICATIONS NETWORK
A CELLULAR TELEPHONE NETWORK, typically based on DIGITAL technologies, which is cheap and reliable enough to compete on price and performance with the conventional telephones now on desks and kitchen walls. The idea is that someday everybody's telephone will sit in their pocket and go everywhere with them. But judging from the teething troubles of the first personal communications networks (PCNS) in the UK – which have

been plagued by lack of capacity and less-than-perfectly reliable technology – someday is still a few years off.

PERSONAL COMPUTER

A computer designed to serve one person only, in contrast to the MAINFRAME or MINICOMPUTER which used MULTI-TASKING operating systems and networks of terminals to serve many people at once. The original personal computers (PCS) were created by hobbyists who were at least as interested in how the machines worked as in what they could do, like the members of Silicon Valley's Homebrew Computer Club, the hang-out of Steve Wozniak and Steve Jobs, founders of APPLE. Most big computer companies turned up their noses at the machines, seeing no advantage over minicomputers or mainframes. They were wrong.

As advances in SEMICONDUCTOR technology have made possible more and more complex microprocessors and cheaper and cheaper MEMORY, both economics and convenience are pushing computing power on to individual's desktops, into their pockets and wherever else it can fit. Many executives now carry in their briefcases more computing power than a 1970s mainframe. They need not follow corporate procedures, or ask permission, to get the resources needed for complex computations, or to create high-quality presentations and letters. They own them. At the same time, networks often enable disparate executives to share information, when they wish to, almost as quickly and conveniently as can be achieved by established procedures. So the personal computer has helped to break down the centrally administered and controlled world of the mainframe in favour of a management style that promotes individual initiative and flexible cooperation.

In 1982 Time *named the personal computer its man of the year.*

P

PGP

Short for Pretty Good Privacy, a freely distributed implementation of the RSA ALGORITHM for public-key encryption, created by Phil Zimmerman. PGP is controversial for several reasons. It has been distributed internationally in defiance of a US export ban on SOFTWARE containing technology for PUBLIC-KEY CRYPTOGRAPHY. It was also distributed without the permission of the holders of the patent on the RSA algorithm. Yet it works and, for those concerned with privacy, PGP is the most secure way of keeping computer DATA from prying eyes.

PHASE

ANALOGUE communications signals are typically built upon CARRIER waves which, as the name suggests, vary rhythmically up and down, positive and negative. Phase refers to where in the cycle – up or down – the wave is. One way of coding INFORMATION into a carrier wave is to alter the phase; that is, to push it up when it would naturally be down.

PHREAKER

A HACKER who concentrates on the telephone system, breaking into corporate voice mail, for example, or using tone-generators to get free international calls. It derives from phone-freak.

PHYSICAL LAYER

That part of the SEVEN LAYER REFERENCE MODEL which concerns the technology used to transmit signals across a communications channel, such as radio waves, electric pulses, light, and so on.

PICT

A technical STANDARD for storing graphics files, commonly used on MACINTOSH personal computers.

PIXEL

Acronym for picture element, or the dots which make up an image on the typical computer screen. Black and white images need only one BIT per pixel, but colour images require that each pixel be represented by a BINARY number. With a BYTE, or eight bits, for each pixel, a screen can contain up to 256 different colours. With 24 bits for each pixel, it can contain 16,777,216 different colours, which is the biggest number 24 bits can express.

PLAIN OLD TELEPHONE SERVICE
See POTS.

PLANNING
The task of formulating a sequence of actions that will achieve some goal: how to get to work, for example, or how to schedule the work of several machine tools to achieve optimal production.

At the heart of most planning systems are actions, that is, things which change the state of the world. Each action is associated with some preconditions, that is, conditions which must be met before the action can be undertaken. In addition, each action also achieves some post-conditions. Planning is mostly a matter of creating a sequence of actions such that each action's pre-conditions are met, and the post-conditions which hold after the completion of the final action are a solution to the problem. This is, of course, easier said than done. But computers have become sufficiently good at the job to schedule production in factories and maintenance for airlines.

PLASMA DISPLAY
A form of computer screen which lights pixels on the screen by passing an electric current through a tiny bubble of gas, causing it to emit light. Plasma screens are compact and bright. But they are also power-hungry and often come in ugly colours.

PLOTTER
A device used for output of line drawings – usually engineering and architectural plans – which typically works by drawing a kind of pen across the surface of a piece of paper.

PLUG COMPATIBLE
A piece of equipment that conforms to the same technical standards as that of another manufacturer. So getting the one to work with the other is as easy as plugging them in. Originally the term referred to a variety of equipment made to work with IBM mainframes, and thus to compete against IBM's versions of the same products.

POINTER
Commonly used in programming, pointers "point" to the location in MEMORY where a piece of DATA is stored.

POLLING
A way of monitoring inputs in which the CPU checks each periodically to see if anything new has arrived. (Contrast to INTERRUPT-driven, in which the inputs demand attention from the CPU.)

POP
Post Office Protocol, a STANDARD for managing the local delivery of E-MAIL from a central server to its many clients. It is used by EUDORA, a popular e-mail program.

POSTSCRIPT
A computer language used to describe to a PRINTER what a page should look like. Postscript was created by John Warnock, who founded Adobe Systems to manufacture and market it. Dr Warnock had worked on computer graphics since his doctoral thesis at the University of Utah, which described quick ways of sketching two-dimensional views of three-dimensional objects. He designed Postscript to be quick and convenient in specifying shapes, fonts, spacing and layout.

Originally he had thought that Postscript would require too much expensive computer MEMORY to work in any but professional typesetting systems. But in 1983 Steve Jobs of APPLE convinced him that memory prices would fall far enough to enable the language to be incorporated into a low-cost LASER PRINTER, like the one Mr Jobs was planning to

launch to accompany his then-forthcoming MACIN-
TOSH computer. This is exactly what they did, and
Dr Warnock spent many sleepless nights worrying
that his fledgling firm would run out of money
before the HARDWARE needed to support his product could be built. In the end Dr Warnock was
rewarded for his bravery with one of the most
consistently profitable products in the history of
computing.

POTS
Short for Plain Old Telephone Service, where you
pick up the phone, dial and speak – no more, no
less.

PowerPC
A design for RISC chips backed by IBM and APPLE for
high-powered personal computers.

Port
Where input or output happens. For example, a
NETWORK port handles DATA coming in from, or
going out to, a network; a PRINTER port handles
traffic for a printer.

PPP
Point to Point Protocol, technical standards that
enable the use of the INTERNET's communication
protocols, TCP/IP, over a dial-up telephone line.
(An alternative to SLIP.)

Activism is the killer app for the Net.
Steven Cherry

PRESENTATION LAYER
That part of the SEVEN LAYER REFERENCE MODEL which
concerns technologies for encryption, COMPRESSION
and encoding DATA being sent across a NETWORK.

PRINTED CIRCUIT BOARD
A way of linking together electronic components
without wires. Printed circuit boards consist of
strips of conducting metal laid on a (non-conduct-

ing) base of epoxy by a process akin to printing. The strips substitute for wires. They typically begin and end in small holes, into which plug stiff wires (called connectors) which protrude from SEMICONDUCTOR chips. Printed circuit boards make it possible to reproduce complex wiring in high volumes at low cost.

PRINTER

A device that enables a computer to output its DATA on to paper. Common types include INK-JET PRINTER, MATRIX PRINTER and LASER PRINTER.

PROCESS

In technology-speak, a process is a running program. In the world of business, a process is some group of activities – typically involving both men and machines – which achieves some goal. Thus there might be a product-delivery process, which gets products to the customer, and a new manager might re-engineer that process in order to achieve the same goals by different (and it is hoped better) means.

PROLOG

See LOGIC PROGRAMMING.

PROM

Short for Programmable, Read-Only Memory, a chip that can store programs or DATA indefinitely. Writing data to a PROM requires special equipment, but once there the data remain even with the power switched off. PROMS are widely used to store and distribute the programs which control electronic devices like modems, calculators and the like. In computers, PROMS typically store the BOOT-STRAP code which enables the machine to find and run its OPERATING SYSTEM (which, in turn, enables it to find and run other programs). (See also EPROM.)

PROTOCOL

A kind of canned dialogue that enables two computers to negotiate, even when they have no idea of the meaning of the symbols that they are sending back and forth. For example, a protocol might specify the sequence of commands which one computer uses to send E-MAIL to another: what to say when a message is coming, how to reply after it has been received, and so on. While humans can make up dialogues as they go along, computers can only stick to the scripts laid down for them in the protocol.

PSTN
Short for Public Switched Telephone Network, a commercial telephone NETWORK.

PTT
Abbreviation for Post, Telephone and Telegraph, usually used to refer to state-owned monopolies which operate most countries' telecommunications, as distinct from the diverse collection of telecoms-service providers which compete for customers in, for example, the USA and the UK.

PUBLIC-KEY CRYPTOGRAPHY
A technology for encrypting messages which overcomes the major weaknesses of earlier codes and ciphers: the difficulty of exchanging a key between coder and decoder. Each code has a key which specifies how the message was encoded, and, in turn, how it can be decoded. Should that key fall into prying hands, the code is useless, hence the plot of many spy novels.

Public-key encryption solves the problem of communicating the key by splitting it into two parts. One part is public, listed in something like a telephone directory. The second is private, and told to nobody. To send a secret message, encrypt the text with the public key of the intended recipient. Then only someone with that person's private key will be able to decode it. Equally a message can be given a DIGITAL SIGNATURE, to ensure that it does indeed come from the person whose name is at the top, by encrypting it with that person's private key, and then decrypting it with the corresponding public key.

The mathematics underlying public-key cryptography is complex, and involves large prime numbers. But so far these are some of the very few encryption techniques that cannot reliably be broken by code-breakers using supercomputers, which is why governments are controversially keen to limit their use. (See also PGP.)

PUNCHED CARD

A computing relic. Instead of disks, early computer programs and DATA were stored by punching holes out of stiff paper cards. Probably the most common card format stored about 80 characters. Cards were read horizontally, like text. The computer determined which number or character was at each position in the text by the vertical location of the hole punched in the cards. While modern programmers complain about a DISK CRASH, old timers know that there are few greater frustrations than dropping a carefully typed deck of cards on to the floor.

In 1947 Tom Watson Sr quashed IBM's plans for its first computer which would store data on magnetic tape because he preferred storing data on punched cards, where it could be seen.

QUERY
Noun or verb describing a request for information to a DATABASE.

QUICKSORT
A commonly used routine to sort DATA into some order: alphabetical, ascending by number, or whatever.

QWERTY
Describes the most popular form of keyboard, which is distinguished by the sequence of keys on the first alphabetic row: q, w, e, r, t and y. Time and motion studies have shown that the layout of the QWERTY keyboard is less than optimal. Characters that frequently occur together in text are placed far apart on the keyboard, forcing unnecessary movement. While more efficient keyboards have been designed, like the Dvorak keyboard, none have yet seriously challenged the dominance of the familiar QWERTY layout.

R

RADIX

The basis of a number system; that is, the number which the system counts in. In a BINARY system the radix is 2, in DECIMAL 10 and in HEXADECIMAL 16.

RAID

Redundant Array of Inexpensive Disks, a way of creating the capacity to store huge quantities of DATA by using a bunch of relatively small disks in unison. The clever trick is stringing the data across the disks so that if one fails a back-up can automatically take its place.

RAM

Short for Random Access Memory, the MEMORY chips used in most computers. RAM stores DATA on an array of transistors. Each element of the array is accessed by location. If the transistor at a given location holds a charge it is interpreted as a BINARY 1, if not then 0.

RAM is quick. Its data can be accessed in billionths of a second, and data can be accessed equally quickly anywhere in the array. RAM is rapidly growing more capacious. By the mid-1990s chips storing over 16m BITS of information were relatively commonplace, and SEMICONDUCTOR laboratories were at work on chips storing over 64m bits. (Simple geometry insists that memory-chip capacity will always grow by multiples of four; if you double the number of circuits that can fit on each side of a rectangle ...)

There are two common sorts of RAM. DRAM is cheap and easy to use, but it requires a constant electric current or it forgets. SRAM is quicker and more permanent, but also more expensive.

RASTER

Describes the most commonly used scheme for the display of text and images on computer screens and printers. Raster screens and printers create lines and images by way of a fixed array of dots, each of which can be coloured, or not, as needed. Early computer screens, and today's plotters, by contrast, displayed images by drawing lines with a pen or electron beam, much as a person would.

The advantage of moving from line to raster, as the arrays of dots are called, is speed of display. It is quick and easy for a computer to scan through a sequence of bytes in MEMORY and colour corresponding dots on screen according to the value found in each BYTE; much quicker and easier than drawing a sequence of lines of varying colour, thickness and orientation.

A disadvantage, however, is that in the transfer to raster form, some lines acquire a stepped, jagged appearance, particularly in low-resolution devices (which use relatively few dots per inch). A second disadvantage is that raster images typically require much more memory to store. Only a few bytes are required to remember the thickness and end points of a line, but to store all the points along and around the line requires much more. But with memory prices continually falling, the speed and convenience of raster technology overshadows its hunger for memory.

REAL NUMBER

Includes both INTEGERS and numbers with a finite number of digits to the right of a decimal point.

REAL TIME

Describes computer systems, usually used to control machinery, which have stringent limits on the time that they can devote to any computation. Most computer systems simply compute until they have finished with a given calculation. The systems helping to navigate a jet fighter, by contrast, cannot ponder their position for too long or the plane will hit something before they are done.

Designers of real-time systems devote much time and energy to calculating in advance just how long any given computation might take, to ensure that it does not disrupt the process of control. This, in turn, breeds a keen appreciation of just how best to balance accuracy and speed in any given situation. Calculating the height of a mountain to greater accuracy offers little reward after the plane has crashed into it. Yet while cruising at altitude an engine control system can profitably devote itself to micro-management of fuel consumption.

RECORD

The basic unit of information stored in a DATABASE. Each record stores all of the information relevant to a particular entry. Databases are composed of records, and records, in turn, are composed of fields, each of which stores part of a record. For example, a customer record might have fields to store name, address, and so on.

RE-ENGINEERING

Rapid, dramatic change to the way a business does its work, typically enabled by the capabilities of new technology. The re-engineering movement's manifesto was an article written in the *Harvard Business Review* by Michael Hammer entitled "Don't Automate, Obliterate". The point of the article was that new technology often enabled work to be done so dramatically differently that many companies would be better off ignoring efforts to improve what they do now, and instead they should simply start over again from scratch.

During the 1990s more and more companies did just that. Three themes ran through their work.

- A shift from sequential work to simultaneous work. With information on paper, only one person can easily access it at a time; on a DATABASE, by contrast, many can do so at once. So many companies are collapsing time-consuming, step-by-step procedures into speedy parallel ones.
- Worker empowerment. The whole point of employing a decision-maker lies in not telling him or her what decisions to make. So managing shifts from telling people what to do to coaching them into higher performance.
- A process view of organisation. Traditionally, managers have thought about how work gets done in their organisations, laying down

detailed procedures for each task. Increasingly re-engineered organisations focus on what is to be done, leaving empowered workers to decide for themselves how these goals can best be met.

REGISTER

Within a MICROPROCESSOR, registers hold the DATA and instructions presently being worked with. The size of the register helps to determine the power and capacity of the microprocessor, for the obvious reason that it determines how much data can be worked on at once. Thus so-called 16-BIT computers have registers that can hold 16 bits at a time; 32-bit computers have registers that can hold 32 bits. By the mid-1990s most personal computers had evolved from the 16-bit registers of the original IBM PC to 32-bit microprocessors, and a few 64-bit machines were beginning to appear.

RELATIONAL DATABASE

Today's most commonly used technology for storing INFORMATION and DATA, the relational database was created by E.F. Codd at IBM in the 1970s. He based the technology on a mathematical theory of relations, which ensured that each piece of data had one, and only one, place in the DATABASE.

Relational databases store information in tables. One or more columns are the index of the table, that is, the key by which information is looked up when needed. Every other piece of data (that is, the other entries on each row) is associated with an index. There are two basic operations on these tables. Filtering the data strips out that which meets (or does not meet) some criteria; for example, all salespeople living in London. A JOIN combines data from different tables. For example, a join between quarterly sales figures (indexed by salesperson's name) and a table of salespeople's addresses (also indexed by name) might be helpful if management wanted to send each salesperson a summary of recent performance.

R

REMOTE PROCEDURE CALL
A PROTOCOL which enables a computer to execute a program on a remote computer, linked across a NETWORK, and then to retrieve the result of that computation.

RENDERING
Describes the process of drawing a surface on a computer graphic. Typically a computer-generated model is built in two steps. A WIRE-FRAME MODEL defines the basic skeleton of the object. Then rendering draws a realistic surface skin over the skeleton to make the object appear to be solid, appropriately textured and appropriately shaded.

RESERVED WORD
One of the words with special meaning in a given programming language. Because reserved words tell the computer to do something, they cannot sensibly be used as names for variables or other DATA. Using a reserved word in programming is a bit like calling a dog Sit, which causes obvious problems in training Sit to sit.

RESET
To return a computer to the state in which it normally finds itself when the power is first switched on. This is a useful last resort when a BUG has caused a program to enter an infinite LOOP, or if for some other reason it will not respond to input.

RGB MONITOR
Red Green Blue monitor, a colour MONITOR that accepts red, green and blue signals separately, and thereby produces sharper images than a COMPOSITE MONITOR, which mixes them together.

RICH TEXT FORMAT
A FILE format created by MICROSOFT to exchange documents between its WORD PROCESSOR, Word, and others, while maintaining fonts, margins and other formatting.

RISC

Short for Reduced Instruction Set Computing, a new philosophy of MICROPROCESSOR design which promises to make much faster and more powerful computers. RISC chips are a tribute to the virtues of simplicity in information technology.

In the 1970s microprocessor designers reasoned that, as most operations are more quickly performed in HARDWARE than in SOFTWARE, the more different functions they could put on to a chip, the faster programs would run. So they devoted their energies to packing more and more functions on to chips.

Then researchers at IBM decided to examine how a representative sample of programs used the functions being packed on to the chips, to see which they should try to optimise. They discovered that programs used intensively only a very small number of relatively simple functions, and did not use many of the more complex instructions at all. Worse, the extra circuitry and rigmarole needed to pack the complex instructions on to the chips slowed the chips down.

So researchers from IBM and elsewhere began designing microprocessors which offered only a very few functions, basically simple arithmetic, comparisons for larger or smaller and manipulating BITS to turn them on or off. Programs grew larger because the new RISC chips required more of their simple instructions to do useful work. But because they devoted all their circuitry to running simple instructions very, very fast, RISC chips were quicker than the CISC chips that preceded them.

In the mid-1990s four different RISC designs led the battle for market share: SUN MICROSYSTEMS' SPARC, IBM'S POWERPC (which was also used by APPLE for a new generation of MACINTOSH computers), Hewlett Packard's Precision architecture and the MIPS chip, backed mostly by workstation-makers like Silicon Graphics. INTEL, for its part, joined with Hewlett Packard to create possible RISC successors to its best-selling range of microprocessors.

ROM

Short for Read-Only Memory; as the name says, MEMORY that can be read but only written using special machinery (usually at the factory). It comes in many formats. Two of the most common are CD-ROM, on compact disks, and PROM, on SEMICONDUCTOR chips. It is considerably more useful than write-only memory.

ROUNDING ERRORS

The arithmetical errors caused by trying to cram real-life numbers, which can have unlimited digits, into the fixed confines of the arbitrary space that most SOFTWARE allocates in computer MEMORY to hold them.

ROUTER

A device which connects two distinct local area networks which use the same technical protocols. (Contrast to BRIDGE, which connects local area networks using different protocols.)

RS-232

RS stands for Requirements Specification in the names of this series of standards for DATA communication created by the USA's Institute of Electrical Engineers. Perhaps the best known of the series is RS-232, which dictates how most personal computers work with modems. The STANDARD lays down such mundane but crucial things as how the MODEM tells the computer it is ready to receive data, how it signals that a connection has been made (or lost), and so on.

RS-422

An improved specification that is gradually replacing RS-232.

RSA ALGORITHM

The most widely used technique for PUBLIC-KEY CRYPTOGRAPHY, named after the initials of its creators, three academics at the Massachusetts Institute of Technology, Rivest, Shamir and Adelman.

RTF
See RICH TEXT FORMAT.

RUN
To execute, for example, a computer program.

RUN-LENGTH ENCODING
A technique for DATA COMPRESSION, which works well on rasterised images and other data which are likely to contain long sequences of the same value. Instead of transmitting a run of, say, 1,000 0s – as might happen in transmitting the all-white background to a rasterised image – run-length encoding transmits an escape character (to denote that coded data follow), then the number of times that the value is repeated, then, finally, the value itself.

For repetitive data, this can shrink dramatically the quantities that need to be transmitted. But for data with little redundancy it can actually increase the quantities transmitted, because denoting one 0 requires more BYTES than simply sending one 0. Run-length encoding is used in FAX machines and many other applications.

S

SCANNER
A device which converts text and images into DI-
GITAL form. Most scanners convert the continuous
tones of a photograph or drawing into an array of
dots, each of which stores the colour at a particular point on the original page. The number of dots
that a scanner stores for each inch of page is
called its optical resolution. Using SOFTWARE to
interpolate new dots between those they have
actually read, many scanners can create the illusion of finer resolution, and thus more detailed
images, than they have actually seen.

SCRIPT
A kind of program. Typically a script is a program
that co-ordinates the work of other programs. So,
for example, a communications script might automate the dialling, LOG-ON and other exchanges
necessary to connect with an ON-LINE DATABASE.
Because they customise existing programs, or
automate small tasks, scripts are typically small
and relatively simple.

SCSI
Short for Small Computer Systems Interface, a
technical STANDARD which enables DISK drives and
other peripherals to be connected to a PERSONAL
COMPUTER.

SECAM
Abbreviation for Séquence Couleur A Mémoire, a
STANDARD for colour television transmission developed in France and used there and in Russia,
among other places. Like PAL it uses 625 lines of
dots to make up a picture, but it codes the
information that makes up the picture differently.

SECURITY
The process of protecting computers and their
DATA from unauthorised access. The three main
aspects of security are as follows.

- **Physical access.** Mainframes and other big
  computers are typically kept in a locked

room to prevent prying or sabotage.
- **SOFTWARE access control.** Each user of a system may be granted, or denied, access to specific files. Passwords and other such mechanisms try to ensure that users really are who they tell the machine they are.
- **Encryption.** Coding data into illegibility can prevent even those who see it from understanding it.

The rapid growth of networks has caught security specialists in a triple bind. Physical access no longer matters much. It is possible to loot a computer in Atlanta from Amsterdam. Software access control schemes do not always work, sometimes because hackers are cleverer than systems designers, but more often because systems administrators are just plain careless. Yet the technology of encryption is only now becoming common and convenient enough to use regularly, and the threat that new PUBLIC-KEY CRYPTOGRAPHY schemes might work all too well is causing governments to consider regulating their use. You just can't win.

Relying on the government to protect your privacy is like asking a peeping tom to install your window blinds.
John Perry Barlow

SEEK TIME

The time required for a DISK to find a piece of DATA; on modern disks typically some thousandths of a second. Disks read and write data on to "cylinders", which run circularly around the surface of the disk, rather like tracks on a vinyl record (except that they do not spiral and they are not incised into the surface). One element of seek time is the time required for the read/write head to move to the proper distance from the centre of the disk; another element is the time then required for the spinning disk to rotate the relevant data to a position under the head.

SEGMENT

A division of MEMORY. Some early microprocessors, including notably those made by INTEL and used in the original IBM PERSONAL COMPUTER, assumed that no program would want to use more than some fixed amount of memory. In Intel's case this was 64 kilobytes, which with hindsight seems a ludicrously small amount. So it created a two-part scheme for finding code and data in memory: one part of the chip specified which segment the processor was then using, while a second specified where in the segment the data lay. This simplified the chip manufacturer's job at the expense of greatly complicating the programmer's, for when programs and data grew larger than 64k, as they quickly did, the complications of keeping track of the different segments were many and annoying.

SEMANTICS

Describes the correspondence between symbols and their meaning. In NERD usage, semantic errors denote the problems of a program which just does the wrong thing, as opposed to syntactic errors, which denote a program that does nothing at all because it has not been written in a form that a computer can understand. In English, "dogs have wings and fly" is a sentence containing semantic errors (because they don't and can't), while "walk dogs tail have and a" is a sentence with syntactic errors (because it is nonsense).

SEMICONDUCTOR

As the name suggests, a material which sometimes conducts electricity; that is, which is neither a conductor, like copper, nor an insulator, like asbestos. Silicon and germanium are good examples. What makes semiconductors so interesting is that, by adding small quantities of impurities called dopants, they can be made into devices which flip from conducting to non-conducting, and thus serve as switches for electrical current. Better still, they can do this very quickly, in a very small space and with no moving parts. Such "solid-state transistors", to use the jargon, form the basis of the silicon chip.

SERIAL
Describes DATA communications in which the BITS travel one after the other, in contrast to PARALLEL COMMUNICATIONS, which send a whole BYTE or word simultaneously.

SESSION LAYER
This part of the SEVEN LAYER REFERENCE MODEL controls synchronisation between interactive computers: which can send what sort of DATA when.

SEVEN LAYER REFERENCE MODEL
A useful abstraction for classifying and organising technical standards for DATA communications, promulgated by the International Standards Organisation. Each level, or layer, handles more and more detailed aspects of communication. By dividing the task into layers, communications technology can be broken up into components, each of which is shielded from changes, problems and complexity at other levels. The seven layers are as follows.

- **PHYSICAL LAYER.** Concerns the electromagnetic signals – electric pulses, radio waves, or light – which carry information across a channel.
- **DATA-LINK LAYER.** Concerns techniques for detecting and correcting errors, and for avoiding conflict when several computers want to access a communications channel at the same time. The data-link layer creates the illusion of a perfect, error-free transmission.
- **NETWORK LAYER.** Concerns the routing of packets from one machine to another across the NETWORK.
- **TRANSPORT LAYER.** Concerns the assembly and disassembly of messages – E-MAIL text, files or whatever – into the packets which are handled by the network layer, and those beneath it.
- **SESSION LAYER.** Adds facilities to the transport layer to handle more interactive applications. The session layer controls which computer can send which messages when, and other

such synchronisation tasks.
- **PRESENTATION LAYER.** Concerns the COMPRES-SION, encryption and coding of data.
- **APPLICATION LAYER.** Concerns the details of converting from the conventions used by one computer system to another; making sure, for example, that data are displayed correctly on the screen, or that file names conform to local naming conventions.

Because, say, the network layer can assume that the data-link layer will transmit its packets – and that it need not worry about how – this separation of responsibilities makes it much easier both to modify networks and to link different sorts of networks. Changes made at the physical layer need not concern any of the "higher" layers, nor need differences between different networks.

SGML
Standard generalised mark-up language, a programming language used to create formatted documents that can be easily transferred between one word processing, or text-formatting, system and another.

SHAREWARE
SOFTWARE that is freely distributed, so as many people as possible can try it out at no cost. Satisfied users are asked to pay a (usually small) fee to the author, and many do. One of the nice things about the on-line world is that it is still possible to make money by trusting in the goodness of your fellow human beings, at least so far.

SHIFT
An operation which moves all the BITS in a word to the right or left. The BYTE 01100101 becomes 00110010 after right-shifting and 11001010 after left-shifting.

SILICON
The form of SEMICONDUCTOR most commonly used in electronic devices.

SIMD
Short for Single Instruction, Multiple Data, a way of organising the processors in a parallel computer. All of the processors work in lockstep, each executing the same instruction at the same time. (Contrast to MIMD, where different processors can execute different instructions.)

SIMM
Short for Single In-line Memory Module, a small PRINTED CIRCUIT BOARD on which are mounted eight or nine MEMORY chips, for ease of installation. Memory chips typically store megabits of DATA, yet computers naturally work in terms of megabytes. By installing eight chips at a time, BITS are turned to BYTES and management is eased. (Nine chips adds an extra for computers which use PARITY to check the contents of memory.)

SIMPLEX
Describes a communications channel which carries DATA in one direction only. (Contrast to DUPLEX.)

SIMPLEX ALGORITHM
A method for calculating optimal solutions to collections of equations. It is commonly used, for example, to minimise time wasted in servicing aircraft or, given a fixed shelf space and demand, to calculate what collection of goods will most likely yield maximum profit. (See also LINEAR PROGRAMMING.)

SLIP
Serial Line Interface Protocol, a version of the INTERNET PROTOCOL adapted for the slow speeds and low reliability of dial-up telephone lines. Together with PPP, SLIP provides an alternative way of getting on to the Internet for those who cannot afford a LEASED LINE.

SMART CARD
A credit-card sized device which contains a MICRO-PROCESSOR and some MEMORY. Smart cards have two potential advantages over ordinary credit cards.

First, they can record the results of a series of transactions, so the card itself knows whether you have exceeded your spending limit, which eliminates the need to call a central DATABASE to verify each transaction. In theory, smart cards could also contain a brief medical history, or any other DATA that a person might want to carry about.

A second potential advantage of smart cards is SECURITY. They can use their intelligence to employ quite sophisticated encryption schemes to protect data they carry, or to work with clever verification protocols to try to ensure that the person using the card is really its owner.

Despite these advantages, however, progress in deploying smart cards has been slow. Part of the difficulty is simply the perennial chicken-and-egg conundrum of introducing new technology: smart cards are not of much use until there are lots of smart-card readers scattered about, and smart-card readers are not of much use until there are lots of people carrying smart cards. But another part of the problem has been the lack of a compelling application. With the growth of networks and electronic shopping, demand for electronic cash may begin to change all that.

SMTP

Simple Mail Transfer Protocol, a set of technical standards for the transfer of E-MAIL from one machine to another. This is the mail PROTOCOL most commonly used on the INTERNET.

SNA

Short for Systems Network Architecture, a grand scheme by IBM to create an over-arching architecture that would incorporate all of the standards necessary to enable a wide variety of different computers and networks to work together. Like many grand schemes it has never been finished, having proved far more complex and difficult than its creators ever imagined.

SNMP

Simple Net Management Protocol, a technical PRO-

S

TOCOL used to manage the operation of machines over a NETWORK: turning them on and off and otherwise making them do things. Perhaps the most famous use of SNMP is the INTERNET toaster. A toaster was connected to the Internet, and people from around the world were invited to control how brown its toast would be; just the sort of senseless technical trick that delights hackers. Despite some effort, the toast delivery problem was never solved.

SOFTWARE
Those information technologies that you cannot drop on your foot, particularly computer programs.

> *Spreadsheets and word processors are the two best-selling types of personal computer software. In 1992 each accounted for about 14% of a US market worth $5.75 billion.*

SOLID STATE DEVICE
An electronic device whose workings depend on the properties of a solid chunk of matter, like the silicon in a silicon chip. This is in contrast to a vacuum tube, which worked by sending electrons across a vacuum. Because they involve no moving parts, and a minimum of mechanical construction, solid-state devices tend to be extremely reliable.

SORT
The process of putting DATA into order: alphabetic, numeric, or whatever. This turns out to be quite tricky to do efficiently, and early computer scientists devoted a great deal of brainpower to devising sorting algorithms. One of the most admired is QUICKSORT, created by Antony Hoare of Oxford University.

SOURCE CODE
The text of a computer program. What a human writes, as opposed to the OBJECT CODE, which is the sequence of 0s and 1s created by a COMPILER from

the source code for a computer to read.

SPAGHETTI CODE

An unstructured computer program. In the early days of computing MEMORY was extremely scarce. As programmers struggled to cram more and more into fewer and fewer lines of code, the logical flow of their programs turned and twisted around itself so intricately as to resemble a bowl of spaghetti, hence the name. Needless to say, spaghetti code is hard to understand and hard to change without breaking. It is generally considered a bad thing.

SPARC

A RISC chip used by SUN MICROSYSTEMS to build its best-selling UNIX WORKSTATION.

SPECIFICATION

A detailed exposition of what a computer system should do. A specification will typically include a description of the business process that is to be automated, the equipment that will be needed to do the job, the screen interfaces through which computers and people will communicate and a step-by-step breakdown of the LOGIC that the program will follow.

In theory, good engineering practice dictates that any significant system have a detailed and accurate specification before writing code. But in practice the ideal is seldom achievable. For one thing, writing specifications is a time-consuming process; the more time spent writing a specification, the greater the risk that the system will be out of date by the time it is delivered. More problematically, to write a detailed specification for a computer system which is meant to change dramatically the way in which work is performed, perhaps as part of a RE-ENGINEERING effort, is to ask people to imagine how work will best be performed in a world unimaginably different from the one in which they now live.

In practice, specifications are often the IT department's first line of bureaucratic defence in a project that is going wrong. "That wasn't in the specification" or "To do that we'd have to rewrite the specification completely" are two phrases often heard when new systems fail to live up to expectations.

SPIRAL MODEL

An approach to building computer systems based on steady, continual improvement rather than a step-by-step progression to a fixed goal. (Contrast to WATERFALL MODEL.)

SPOOLING

A technique to make more convenient communication between a computer and a PERIPHERAL device. Spooling uses a BUFFER to store temporarily any DATA that the quicker machine might send in advance of the slower one's ability to consume it. That way the quicker machine need not be always waiting for the slower one to catch up.

It is ultimately unworthy for excellent men to lose hours like slaves in the labour of calculation which could safely be relegated to anyone else if machines were used.
G.W. Leibnitz, 1685

SPREADSHEET

One of the applications that made the PERSONAL COMPUTER popular. Spreadsheets are an automated version of the arrays of figures used by accountants to make financial calculations. Many rows or columns in such spreadsheets are calculated from previous rows or columns, according to relatively simple formulae. In the automated version, the user enters the formula directly into the spreadsheet and the computer keeps the calculations up to date even if the numbers change.

The idea for the spreadsheet is said to have come to Dan Bricklin – an entrepreneur who created VisiCalc, the first spreadsheet, for the APPLE II computer – as he sat in a class at the Harvard Business School, pondering a particularly tedious blackboard-full of numbers. His idea sold millions of computers. It is also said that spreadsheets fuelled the takeover boom of the 1980s by making it easy to perform the tedious calculations needed to value a company under various assumptions of its future earnings.

SQL

Structured query language, the programming language most commonly used for asking questions of databases. It was originally developed by IBM. In theory, it offers a kind of *lingua franca* for databases; SQL can be used to access any DATA from any DATABASE that understands the language. Most databases nowadays speak SQL. Unfortunately, however, there are several competing dialects.

SRAM

See STATIC RANDOM ACCESS MEMORY.

STACK

A way of storing incoming and outgoing DATA in MEMORY which operates on a LIFO, or last-in, first-out, basis.

STANDARD

Like OPEN SYSTEM, another much abused phrase in computing. Strictly, a standard is a technical specification agreed by a national or international standard-setting body, like ANSI or the ISO. In computer-industry practice, however, standard-setting bodies often move too slowly to keep up with technology. So many widely accepted technologies become established as *de facto* standards. Instead of a single, detailed technical specification, like that created by a standards-setting body, *de facto* standards are typically created by copying the behaviour of the most popular version of the technology, or simply buying a copy of it. The hope of creating a *de facto* standard like MICROSOFT'S DOS has in turn inspired marketers and advertisers to proclaim every new product a "standard". These days, it does not require too much cynicism to equate the phrase "emerging new standard" with "over-hyped, unproven, new product".

STANDARD GENERALISED MARK-UP LANGUAGE

See SGML.

START BIT

A BIT sent in many communications protocols to denote the start of a new character.

STATIC RANDOM ACCESS MEMORY

A form of RAM. Like DRAM it stores the 0s and 1s of BINARY DATA as electric charges in the rows and columns of a grid of circuits. Unlike DRAM its circuits will hold their charge indefinitely; they do not need to be constantly refreshed. This makes static memory faster and more reliable than DRAM, but also much more expensive.

STOP BIT

A BIT sent in many communications protocols to denote the end of a character.

STORE AND FORWARD

A simple way of constructing a computer NET-WORK. Each computer has a rough map of the machines to which it is connected. When it receives a message it decides – guessing if necessary – which of the machines to which it is connected is closer to the message's destination. Then it stores the message until it has a connection to that machine, and sends it on. This technique was the basis of FIDONET, USENET and other early do-it-yourself networks.

STREAM

A general way of referring to the things inside a computer that generate or receive DATA. An input or output port can be a stream. But so can, say, the part of a program that generates a list of random numbers.

STRING

Techno-term for a piece of text, or any other string of characters in a row.

S

STRUCTURED PROGRAMMING

A 1970s panacea, which is still proving itself very useful in the 1990s, even if it is not the answer to all an automator's woes. The basic idea behind structured programming is that computer programs, like machinery, should be composed of a collection of discrete components, each of which performs a specific and well-defined function.

Use of structured programming was often accompanied by a complementary approach to problem solving, called top-down decomposition. The idea is to state the basic steps of a solution simply and at a fairly high level of abstraction. Then do the same for the steps of the steps, and so on, until a level of detail is reached that can be written as a computer program.

The basic component of a structured program is called a SUBROUTINE, and collections of related subroutines are often further differentiated by collecting them into modules. Modules are crucial for large programming projects. By dividing work into more or less independent chunks, they enable even large teams to work together without tripping over each other's feet.

The biggest difficulty with structured programming is that, unlike the promises made by some of its early promoters, it does not solve all of the problems of the known universe. Some problems do not lend themselves to neat top-down decomposition. While structured programming enabled programmers to create larger, more complex programs than they did before, really big programs still defeat it.

STRUCTURED QUERY LANGUAGE

See SQL.

SUBROUTINE

A basic component of a computer program; a small piece of code that does a specific job.

SUN MICROSYSTEMS

The leading manufacturer of UNIX WORKSTATIONS.

SWAPPING

See VIRTUAL MEMORY.

SYMBOL-PROCESSING HYPOTHESIS

The idea underlying most approaches to ARTIFICIAL INTELLIGENCE that intelligent activity can take place as the manipulation of symbols alone, without regard to their underlying meaning. A critical thought experiment to test the hypothesis is the "Chinese room" proposed by a philosopher, John Searle. The Chinese room works roughly as follows. In an isolated room lives a man equipped with a dictionary and a stock of tiles, each imprinted with a Chinese ideogram. Each entry in the dictionary relates one ideogram to another ideogram. In the morning the man is presented with a tray containing columns of ideograms. His task, over the course of the day, is to replace each ideogram with its corresponding entry from the dictionary. The man has no idea what any of the ideograms mean. The question is, is he "thinking"? Discuss this at your next dinner party.

SYNCHRONOUS

Having clocks ticking in unison, as opposed to ASYNCHRONOUS, where no attempt is made to keep clocks on the same time. When clocks tick in unison, there is no need to add extra machinery to communications protocols to synchronise two machines, like stop bits. But keeping clocks ticking in unison is typically more trouble than it is worth.

SYNTAX

Concerning grammatical structure, in contrast to SEMANTICS, which concerns meaning. Most errors in programs concern syntax: a missing comma here, or a mis-spelled variable name there. Fortunately, syntactic errors are usually easy for the COMPILER to detect and warn the programmer about. The really dangerous errors are where the program makes perfect sense, but not the sense that the programmer intended.

S

SYSTEMS ADMINISTRATION

The management of computer systems: includes setting up user accounts, running networks, repairing and recovering from errors, installing and configuring SOFTWARE, backing-up DATA and a host of other tasks, many of them thankless.

SYSTEMS ANALYSIS

The process of discovering and documenting how business processes work, and defining how computers can (it is hoped) make them work better.

T

TAPE DRIVE
Tape cartridges are commonly used for back-up and archival storage of computer DATA. They can hold a lot of data (150 megabyte tapes are relatively common) and the technology is well understood and reasonably cheap. But tapes are also slow and vulnerable to snarling. As the technology matures, the tape drive is gradually being replaced by the OPTICAL DISK.

TCP/IP
The NETWORK protocols used on the INTERNET. It stands for TRANSMISSION CONTROL PROTOCOL and INTERNET PROTOCOL.

TDMA
Short for Time Division Multiple Access, another name for TIME DIVISION MULTIPLEXING.

TELEPRESENCE
The feeling of being there that people get from a well-crafted VIRTUAL REALITY program. More often used to describe the lack of feeling of being there given by most of today's virtual reality programs.

TELETYPE
The simplest form of TERMINAL, in which text, and only text, is sent to the screen character by character, line by line, with only the simplest of formatting. When a line fills, the next one is started. When a screen fills, it scrolls up one line. MICROSOFT's original DOS for the PERSONAL COMPUTER offered a teletype INTERFACE, and Microsoft is now making billions selling WINDOWS SOFTWARE to make the machines easier and prettier to use. (Contrast to GRAPHICAL USER INTERFACE.)

TELNET
The process which enables someone to log-in to a remote computer and use its services via the INTERNET. Contrast to FTP, which enables a person to get DATA from a remote computer, or REMOTE PROCEDURE CALL, which enables a program to access the services of a remote computer.

TERA-

A terabyte is about 1 trillion BYTES. Strictly, because computers count in powers of two rather than powers of ten, 1,099,511,627,766 bytes, or bits. (See also KILO-, MEGA- and GIGA-.)

TERMINAL

A screen and keyboard which enable a person to communicate with a computer. Also used loosely to refer to a personal computer when it is used largely to communicate with a minicomputer or mainframe.

TERMINAL EMULATION

SOFTWARE which helps personal computers to communicate more effectively with large ones. In addition to managing communication, the software enables the smaller machines to understand the "magic" commands which position the CURSOR on the screen, or make characters stand out in bold.

TIFF

Tagged Image File Format, a technical STANDARD often used for storing graphics files on both UNIX machines and personal computers.

TIME DIVISION MULTIPLEXING

A way of allowing many different communications streams to share the same communications channel. Each is allocated its own series of time slots to keep it from becoming confused with the others. (See MULTIPLEX.)

TIME SHARING

The process of allowing many people and programs to use the same computer simultaneously. Each in turn gets a few milliseconds of time on the central processor to calculate. Because the switching is so fast, and takes clever advantage of the inevitable delays in input and output, it usually – but not always – appears that each has its own computer. (See also MULTI-TASKING.)

TLA
Three Letter Acronym, seemingly the technologist's favourite form of communication.

TOKEN RING
A popular way of managing the flow of DATA across a LOCAL AREA NETWORK. A simple discipline prevents computers from sending data at the same time and so garbling each other's messages. The computers continually pass a kind of electronic token from one to another, in order. Computers only send data when they hold the token. This is in contrast to ETHERNET, the other popular way of managing the flow of data across local area networks, which simply detects collisions between data, and requires the computers involved to send again (after each has waited for a random interval, to prevent the collision from happening a second time).

The extra overhead of passing the token means that token-ring networks are somewhat slower than Ethernet at light loads. But they can be less easily overwhelmed by heavy loads than Ethernet, and so are popular for factory AUTOMATION, and other applications where the volume of data traffic varies widely and assured performance is crucial.

TRANSISTOR
An electronic switch, which is turned on (conducting electricity) or off (not conducting electricity) by the application of a small electric current.

Moore's Law. The number of transistors that can be etched on to a given area of silicon doubles every 18 months.

TRANSMISSION CONTROL PROTOCOL
The TCP in TCP/IP, these technical standards determine how messages are broken up into packets for transmission over the INTERNET – using the INTERNET PROTOCOL – and reassembled again at the other end. In terms of the SEVEN LAYER REFERENCE

MODEL, TCP corresponds to the TRANSPORT LAYER.

TRANSPORT LAYER

That part of the SEVEN LAYER REFERENCE MODEL which concerns standards for how communications – the text of an E-MAIL, say – should be assembled and disassembled for transmission over a PACKET NETWORK.

TROJAN HORSE

A program used to capture unsuspecting people's log-ons and passwords. Typically a Trojan horse looks like the screen ordinarily presented when first logging on to a computer. But, unlike the usual screen, it records the LOG-ON and PASSWORD – where the creator of the Trojan horse can later retrieve them – before allowing the user to go about his or her business.

TTY

See TELETYPE.

TURING MACHINE

A simple, abstract model of a computer used in computing theory to show what a machine can and cannot do.

TURING TEST

A test of intelligence proposed by Alan Turing, a British mathematician and computer-science pioneer. A computer could be truly said to be intelligent, Turing proposed, on the day that it could hold a conversation with a person, and trick that person into thinking that it was one of them. Appearance need not matter; the conversation could occur by typing at a TERMINAL. But knowledge of language, common sense, reasoning ability and, probably, a sense of humour, would matter greatly.

Turing predicted computers would pass his test by the millennium. No chance. Hugh Loebner, a producer of lighted plastic disco dance-floors, has sponsored an annual Turing-test competition since 1991. A panel of judges converses with several terminals, each of which is connected to either a person or a machine. So far, telling one from the other has been as easy as telling night from day. Even if they try, few people can manage to be as monumentally stupid as a computer.

> *Not until a machine can write a sonnet or compose a concerto because of thoughts and emotions felt, and not by the chance fall of symbols, could we agree that machine equals brain.*
> Sir Geoffrey Robinson, 1949

TWAIN
Short for Tool Without an Interesting Name, a STANDARD for exchanging DATA between a SCANNER and the software that makes use of the scanned images.

TWISTED PAIR
The kind of wiring used in the telephone system; typically, as the name suggests, two copper wires twisted one around the other. Contrast to COAXIAL CABLE, which consists of a single, larger copper wire surrounded by shielding to prevent electromagnetic interference.

U

UART
Short for Universal Asynchronous Receiver/Transmitter, which usually refers to the chip that encodes and decodes DATA for transmission over the telephone line. In general, it denotes any chip that converts the parallel data STREAM within a computer into a SERIAL one, and vice versa.

UNIVERSAL RESOURCE LOCATOR
See URL.

UNIVERSAL SERVICE
Strictly, universal service is a noble goal that motivates the world's telephone companies: to give everyone the ability to communicate. In practice, universal service is also widely tied to a system of cross-subsidies that is coming into increasing conflict with the two forces now driving the transformation of telecoms markets: technological change and market competition.

The creators of the first telephone networks had two problems in setting prices that everyone could afford. First, laying wires to remote rural locations cost more than wiring cities. Second, the cost structure of the telephone network, in which most costs were the fixed costs of NETWORK investment, translated awkwardly into pricing structures that homeowners and other small users could afford. Setting monthly or quarterly line rentals high enough to recover fixed costs would deter many homeowners from getting on to the network. Yet homeowners also did not talk on the telephone much, so they would not pay for themselves in per-minute charges either.

The telephone companies set up a system of cross-subsidies. As monopolies they could charge what they liked. So they charged relatively high prices to business and long-distance users, and used the profits to cover losses on residential customers. Governments, in turn, codified the system of cross-subsidies in telecoms rate regulations.

But today that system, which worked comfortably for half a century, is falling apart. New competitors are entering telecoms markets, and new technologies are creating new services. New questions bedevil telephone companies and their regulators. Who should pay extra for universal service? Which services should pay over the odds? Which should be subsidised? Not only are the questions hard to answer, but, worse, in doing so regulators second-guess the market. Instead of encouraging competition and innovation, they crush it by setting prices that favour one political constituency over another.

Finding new means to achieve the goal of universal service promises to be one of the biggest regulatory challenges for the remainder of the decade. In the USA, one proposed solution is to levy a tax on all telecoms companies to subsidise "deserving" people (whoever they may be deemed to be). In the UK, some people are talking about trying to do away with cross-subsidies altogether. Whatever solution is adopted will have a huge impact on the telecoms revolution, for better, for worse, or both.

In the first computer forecast of an election result, a UNIVAC computer predicted that Eisenhower would win by a wide margin in 1952. But broadcasters at CBS, whose election-night gimmick it was, did not believe the machine and fudged the results to be in line with conventional polls. The polls were wrong; the machine was right.

UNIX

Probably the most influential piece of SOFTWARE ever invented, Unix is a MULTI-TASKING OPERATING SYSTEM originally created at AT&T's Bell Laboratories in the early 1970s. At the time AT&T was the USA's regulated telephone monopoly, and so forbidden from competing in computer markets. It therefore freely distributed Unix, together with its source code, to universities. For two decades, computer-science students have had their impressions of what a computer should look like shaped by Unix. At the same time they have used it as the

U

foundation on which new innovations have been built.

The INTERNET is built on Unix, via the networking facilities added to the operating system at the University of California at Berkeley in the late 1970s. The design of MICROSOFT'S DOS, the most popular operating system for personal computers, owes a large intellectual debt to Unix. The most popular programming language for small computers, C, was developed in conjunction with Unix. Unix's design philosophy – that computer programs should be small and designed to do a specific task well – has informed a generation of programmers, and created a host of small-but-useful tools for the programming community.

For most of its history, however, Unix's intellectual impact has overshadowed its actual use. It was adopted and extended by hackers, which made it hard for ordinary mortals to use. The hackers themselves have fought bitterly over different versions of Unix, fragmenting the market. The two main camps have been AT&T's own version of Unix, called System V, and descendants of the version of Unix created at the University of California at Berkeley, called BSD (for Berkeley System Distribution).

Today, however, with the growth of networks, Unix is making steady inroads into the corporate world. SUN MICROSYSTEMS, the leading maker of the UNIX WORKSTATION, has tried to reconcile Berkeley Unix and System V with yet another new version of the operating system, called Solaris. While it seems unlikely that Unix will start popping up on desktops, it may yet become the glue that holds corporate networks together, managing both databases and communications across companies and the world.

UNIX WORKSTATION

A relatively high-powered desktop computer which runs the UNIX OPERATING SYSTEM. In the late 1980s Unix workstations were almost exclusively used for demanding computing tasks like COMPUTER AIDED DESIGN and scientific research. But as personal computers become more powerful – and equipped with lots of MEMORY and high-resolution screens – high-end PCS increasingly compete for desktop tasks, while Unix workstations, in turn, are increasingly used to manage networks, as the FILE SERVER and in other back-room chores formerly done by a MINICOMPUTER.

UPLOAD
To send DATA "up" from a small computer to a larger one. (Contrast to DOWNLOAD.)

URL
Short for Universal Resource Locator, an address describing the location of a document, computer program or other resource used by the WORLD WIDE WEB. URLS are the Web's way of finding things.

USENet
USENET is the world's largest conversation. It consists of over 10,000 news groups, each using E-MAIL to discuss a specific topic, from *alt.sex*, unsurprisingly the most popular NEWS GROUP, to *comp.unix.wizards*, which provides technical advice on the more arcane features of the UNIX OPERATING SYSTEM.

The evolution of the USENET is an excellent example of why today's computer networks are different from yesterday's telephone ones. USENET was built from the bottom up. When Unix was first distributed to universities it had little technical documentation. To hackers interested in networks, however, this problem became an opportunity. To share technical information among hackers, they devised the UUCP communications PROTOCOL to enable far-flung hackers to talk to each other via their machines, using a STORE AND FORWARD approach. Thus USENET was born.

More recently, USENET has adopted INTERNET protocols to transmit messages. Today, the two biggest issues facing the USENET are over-popularity and censorship. Many news groups have become so popular that NOISE is beginning to drown out signal. At the same time, concerns over pornography have led some universities to ban the less socially redeeming news groups, like *alt.sex.bestiality.*

UUCP
Unix to Unix Copy Protocol, a way of moving files and E-MAIL from one UNIX machine to another. It is now largely superseded by SMTP and other INTERNET protocols.

UUENCODE
Together with uudecode, provides a way of sending programs and other BINARY files via E-MAIL. The problem that they solve concerns the number of BITS transmitted reliably. In binary files, all eight bits in each BYTE are crucial; in text files only the last seven really matter. In a short-sighted attempt to make them simple, some e-mail systems were designed in such a way that they do not transmit the eighth bit reliably. So uuencode and uudecode are used to translate binary files into a form which can be sent by e-mail, and back again. On the MACINTOSH, a program called BINHEX does the same thing.

V STANDARDS

A collection of technical standards set by the CCITT for modems.

Standard	Description
V.21	For DATA communications at 300 BITS per second. In the USA Bell 103A is more commonly used.
V.22	For data communications at 1,200 bits per second. In the USA Bell 212A is more common.
V.22 *bis*	For data communications at 2,400 bits per second.
V.32	For data communications at 4,800 or 9,600 bits per second.
V.32 *bis*	For data communications at 14,400 bits per second.
V.42	For error-checking and reducing line NOISE.
V.42 *bis*	For compressing data for faster transmission.
V.FAST	For data communications at 28,800 bits per second.

VAX

A brand of MINICOMPUTER made by DIGITAL EQUIPMENT CORPORATION. Vaxes (or Vaxen, as they are sometimes known) were the hot computer of the late 1970s and early 1980s. But the role of mini-computers in general, and Vaxes in particular, has since been steadily eroded by the PERSONAL COMPUTER and UNIX WORKSTATION.

VALUE-ADDED NETWORK

A communications NETWORK which does more – and typically costs more – than the ordinary public switched network. More could mean higher BANDWIDTH, improved DATA-carrying capabilities, or just about anything an engineer can dream up.

VAPOURWARE

SOFTWARE that exists only in the marketing brochure. The software industry is notorious for announcing new products long in advance in the hope of deterring customers from buying a rival's product. Some long-promised products have never materialised.

VECTOR GRAPHICS
Refers to graphics in which the computer remembers the shapes by a description of their geometry – the line segments that make up the figures – rather than simply a BIT MAP of its representation on a particular screen.

VIRTUAL MEMORY
A technique for enabling a computer to work as if it had more DRAM than is in fact installed in the machine. The trick is to swap the contents of a chunk of MEMORY on to the HARD DISK, and substitute for it something that will be needed sooner. The key, obviously, is to ensure that the stuff written to disk is not immediately read back in again (a research topic which has been the subject of many doctoral theses).

Often virtual memory is managed by organising memory into standard-sized chunks, called pages. The swapping of pages into and out of memory is, not surprisingly, called PAGING.

VIRTUAL PRIVATE NETWORK
A service offered by telephone service providers enabling big companies to tie together far-flung facilities into an apparently seamless network, which can be managed as easily and flexibly as if all the telephones were linked to the same PABX.

VIRTUAL REALITY
Imaginary worlds created by the use of high-powered computing technology. Virtual reality has been hyped as the ultimate extension of the human senses. It might, someday, enable people to work in worlds they could not otherwise experience; for example, to visualise the world inside a human vein, or to manipulate simulated molecules to help in developing more effective drugs. It might also enable people to create new worlds of the imagination. One pioneer of virtual reality research created an undersea world in which she lived and

moved as a lobster (your fantasies may differ).

Today, however, the reality is more prosaic. The technology of virtual reality has three key components, each of which has much room for improvement.

- **Headsets.** In order to create the illusion of a three-dimensional world, virtual reality presents slightly different images to each eye using a head-covering pair of goggles. Today's are still heavy and clumsy.
- **Simulations.** To recreate an imaginary world, computers must be able to calculate how the world works: how bodies move and stretch; how much resistance to force they offer; how they break apart.
- RENDERING. In addition to calculating how the world works, virtual reality must make it look right. This requires the computer to create realistic-looking surfaces, textures and colours, which in turn requires brain boggling quantities of computing power.

In addition to getting the technology right, the elements must be combined in ways to convince the subtly sensitive human brain. A problem yet to be overcome with goggles, for example, is that goggle eyes in fact focus only a few inches in front of the face. This gives a feeling of claustrophobia instead of an illusion of depth.

VIRUS

A self-replicating and often malicious computer program. A virus typically stitches its code into that of another program. Each time that program is executed in a new machine, the virus looks for a way of infecting that computer as well.

Once it has infected a machine, the virus awaits some date or signal to work its mischief. Friday the 13th is a popular day for triggering viruses. So is Michelangelo's birthday. Once triggered, some viruses wreak havoc, say by deleting all files on a HARD DISK. Others merely annoy, by flashing messages on the screen.

To avoid infection by viruses, it is best to practice "safe computing". Avoid borrowing or sharing programs (especially with strangers), although data should usually be innocuous. Run an ANTI-VIRAL program frequently to try to detect infection before damage occurs.

VISION

Giving a computer vision is in one sense just a matter of hooking up a video camera. But getting it to see requires the machine to make sense of the images which the camera presents. As in so many areas of artificial intelligence, what seems trivially easy for people turns out to be desperately difficult for machines.

Part of the problem is that people bring knowledge to bear on the problem of visual understanding that machines utterly lack. When a person views, say, a factory conveyor belt, he already knows that it is likely to carry parts which are distinct from the belt, which move with it and which cast shadows. He uses this knowledge to distinguish the parts of the scene. Machines, which lack this knowledge, just get confused.

Recently, however, researchers have begun having more success in computer vision by trying to train computers just to react to visual inputs – rather than to try to "understand" them. In the retina of a frog, for example, nerve cells are wired together so that they are highly stimulated by small, moving objects – like a fly. The cells react even before the frog has a chance to think about what he might be throwing his tongue at. By wiring up neural nets to mimic the instinctive reactions of nerve cells, researchers are teaching computers to recognise a variety of sights. One such, at Carnegie Mellon University, has been trained to recognise the road before a moving car – and reacts in such a way that it does a pretty good job of driving.

VMS

The proprietary OPERATING SYSTEM used by DIGITAL EQUIPMENT CORPORATION'S VAX computers.

VON NEUMANN BOTTLENECK

The motivation for parallel computing. Computers derived from the basic conceptual designs laid down in the 1950s by John von Neumann, a scientist at Princeton University, have a fundamental limitation. They each have a CPU which executes instructions stored in main MEMORY, together with the data they work on. The faster the CPU works, the greater the percentage of its processing time it spends simply fetching instructions from memory. At some point, all of the increase in speed is consumed simply gathering instructions rather than doing the work which those instructions dictate.

One way to lessen the impact of the bottleneck is to use a CACHE. The idea is to try to anticipate which instructions will be needed next – which is often easy to do, for programs are often read sequentially – and move those instructions to an area of the central processor, called a cache, from which they can be quickly fed into the actual computing machinery. A theoretically better solution, however, is to have several processors working simultaneously, or PARALLEL PROCESSING.

VRAM

Video RAM, a type of computer MEMORY designed so that its contents can be simultaneously read (by a display screen) and written to (by the central processor). Most conventional forms of RAM cannot do both at once. Simultaneous access enables quicker, smoother graphics displays.

VSAT

Very Small Aperture Terminal, a communications satellite whose transmissions cover only a very small area of the earth beneath them. A smaller footprint means less risk of interference, and hence less need for regulation.

VULCAN NERVE PINCH

The keyboard command that makes a computer stop what it is doing and reset itself. In DOS it involves holding down the Control, Alt and Delete keys simultaneously.

WAIS

Short for Wide Area Information Service, a set of programs that tries to make available INFORMATION widely scattered across the INTERNET. WAIS allows people to search the world's documents for information on a given subject, and progressively narrow the search to those relevant just to them. Although the potential is vast, growth in the use of WAIS has been slow, partly because it requires time-consumingly prepared indexes to the DATA before it can be accessed.

WAN

See WIDE AREA NETWORK.

WATERFALL MODEL

The traditional way of developing a computer system, in which each step – from design to testing – follows one after the other. The problem with the waterfall model, and the reason why fewer and fewer programs are being built this way, lies in the delays it creates. Creating programs step by step can often take four or five years. Given the speed of change in the business world, this can often make programs irrelevant by the time they are completed.

WEB BROWSER

SOFTWARE which makes it possible to view the global HYPERMEDIA that make up the WORLD WIDE WEB, and to follow the links between documents. NETSCAPE is the most popular; MOSAIC, from which Netscape was derived, is the second-most popular.

WEB MASTER

The person who manages a computer linked to the WORLD WIDE WEB.

WETWARE

The most traditional of computing technologies: the human brain. (Contrast to HARDWARE and SOFTWARE.)

W

WIDE AREA INFORMATION SERVICE
See WAIS.

WIDE AREA NETWORK
A NETWORK which links distant machines. Typically at least part of a wide area network (WAN) traverses the PSTN; that is, it involves DATA carried by a telephone company.

WINDOW
Generically a window is a computer screen within a screen. It is a separate area that can show an entirely different view from other windows, which updates its text and/or graphics independently of other windows, and which can be adjusted in size independently of other windows.

WINDOWS
MICROSOFT's best-selling "operating environment". Windows sits on top of DOS, the nearly ubiquitous OPERATING SYSTEM for IBM-COMPATIBLE computers, from whence it provides an easy-to-use graphical INTERFACE, the ability to hold several programs in MEMORY simultaneously and other convenient features. Microsoft is now trying to expand usage of the Windows interface to everything from television remote controls to supercomputers.

WIRE-FRAME MODEL
The skeleton which underlies most computer generated images and specifies the basic shape of the object. To complete the graphical illusion, RENDERING covers the wire-frame model with a realistic-looking surface.

WORD PROCESSOR
A program that edits text.

WORKFLOW
SOFTWARE designed to help manage the progress of work through an office. It typically helps to keep track of deadlines. It notes the order of the steps in which a task must be accomplished, and helps to ensure that work flows down its pre-ordained

path. It can also help keep track of who must authorise a given piece of work.

Proponents of workflow point out that, by helping to prompt workers through complex tasks, it can ease the problems of coping with complex tasks and fast-paced, quick-changing office procedures. Critics, by contrast, argue that even relatively simple office work has more subtleties than can be easily expressed to a computer. So the efficiency of workflow systems comes only at the expense of rigidity.

Roughly 90% of those cruising the World Wide Web are male; most are in their 20s and 30s.

WORLD WIDE WEB

The technology that makes the INTERNET usable by mere humans, the World Wide Web (WWW) is a system of HYPERMEDIA linking text, graphics, sound and video on computers spread across the globe.

The basic technology of the web was originally created by Tim Berners-Lee at CERN, Europe's atom-smasher sited near Geneva, to help physicists keep track of all the DATA generated by their experiments. At the heart of the technology is a programming language, HTML, which allows a phrase or graphic in one document to be linked to another document anywhere on the global Internet. When a person clicks a MOUSE on that highlighted phrase, the linked document is fetched and brought to the screen automatically.

Refinements to the technology of the Web have in fact expanded the use of links beyond simply fetching pre-existing documents. A LINK can also trigger a computer program which creates a document, say by querying a DATABASE. Or it can bring to the screen a form, to be filled in interactively. Or it can launch E-MAIL. In this way, the Web is rapidly becoming an easy-to-use, general-purpose INTERFACE for the Internet and the computers on it.

Many companies are putting up Web sites to provide information about their products. Others are using the technology to sell goods directly over the NETWORK, in a kind of electronic mail-order. The World Wide Web could prove to be the SOFTWARE that brings the Internet to the masses, and vice versa.

WORM

Write Once, Ready Many, a form of storage that writes DATA irreversibly to a DISK, typically an OPTICAL DISK. It is useful for archival storage, but not much else.

WORM

A program that propagates itself across a NETWORK, automatically transferring itself to distant machines and running itself there (from whence it transfers itself to more machines). In contrast to a VIRUS, which secretes itself inside another program – and thus is only spread when the program carrying it is spread – worms take charge of their own reproduction. Perhaps the most famous worm was created by a computer science student called Robert Morris in 1988. In what seems to have been a misguided attempt to map the global INTERNET, Morris created a worm which replicated itself so rapidly that it brought thousands of computers to a standstill.

WWW

See WORLD WIDE WEB.

X.25

An international technical STANDARD for PACKET-SWITCHED DATA networks.

X.400

An international STANDARD for the transport of E-MAIL; an alternative to SMTP.

X.500

An international STANDARD for E-MAIL addresses, and directories. The goal of x.500 is to make it easy to find any e-mail address, easier even than getting a telephone number. Like many international standards, however, it grew almost unusably unwieldy in the drafting, as each special interest added its little bit, and so is as yet little used.

XENIX

A version of UNIX (System V) developed by MICROSOFT for use on personal computers.

XMODEM

A FILE-transfer PROTOCOL widely used on personal computers.

XON-XOFF

These two signals form a widely used way of controlling the flow of DATA across a communications line. When the receiving computer is getting more data than it can handle, it sends a xoff to the sender, which causes it to pause in transmission until a xon is sent.

XOR

Also called exclusive OR, this is an operation on two BITS which returns a 1 if and only if the bits are not equal (that is, if one bit is 1 and the other is 0). (Contrast to OR, which returns a 1 if the bits are not equal and also if they are both 1.)

X WINDOWS

The GUI most commonly used on UNIX. Developed at MIT, X, as it is commonly called, provides Unix

users with many of the conveniences of a MACIN-
TOSH: resizable windows on the screen to show
different views of DATA, a MOUSE to point and click
with, menus to choose commands from, and so
on.

YMMV

Your Mileage May Vary, a phrase often used in E-MAIL to indicate that, well, your mileage may vary; that is, what works for me might not always work as well for you.

YMODEM

Yet another FILE-transfer PROTOCOL, commonly used on personal computers.

Z

Z39.50

A technical STANDARD used to manage bibliographic information scattered across the networks. Z39.50 covers both the indices with which the DATA is organised, and the sort of queries that can be asked of it.

ZEROTH

A HACKER's term for first.

ZIP

A way of compressing files widely used on IBM-COMPATIBLE personal computers. Files so compressed are by convention denoted by the suffix .zip.

ZMODEM

Yet another FILE-transfer PROTOCOL for personal computers.

ZONE

A group of computers on a NETWORK. In a company each department might have its own zone, which is administered more or less independently from the rest. The obvious advantage of zones is that breaking up administrative problems into small pieces lessens their complexity, if only by making it harder for an administrator in one zone to inadvertently mess up another's computers.

Part 3
APPENDIXES

1 Abbreviations and acronyms

ACK	Acknowledgement
ADSL	Asynchronous Digital Subscriber Loop
AI	Artificial Intelligence
ASCII	American Standard Code for Information Interchange
ATM	Asynchronous Transfer Mode
BASIC	Beginner's All-purpose Symbolic Instruction Code
BIT	Binary Digit
BTW	By The Way
CAD	Computer Aided Design
CALS	Computer Aided Logistics and Support
CAM	Computer Aided Manufacturing
CASE	Computer Aided Software Engineering
CCIT	French-language acronym for International Consultative Committee for Telephony and Telegraphy
CDMA	Code Division Multiple Access
CD-ROM	Compact Disk, Read-Only Memory
CGI	Common Gateway Interface
CIM	Computer Integrated Manufacturing
CIO	Chief Information Officer
CISC	Complex Instruction Set Computing
CMOS	Complementary Metal Oxide Semiconductor
COBOL	Common Business Oriented Language
CORBA	Common Object Request Broker Architecture
CPU	Central Processing Unit
CRC	Cyclic Redundancy Check
CSCW	Computer Supported Co-operative Work
DBMS	Database Management System
DEC	Digital Equipment Corporation
DOS	Disk Operating System
DRAM	Dynamic Random Access Memory
E-mail	Electronic Mail
EBCDIC	Enhanced Binary Coded Decimal

	Interchange Code
EDI	Electronic Data Interchange
EISA	Extended Industry Standard Architecture
EMACS	Editing Macros
EOF	End Of File
EPROM	Erasable, Programmable, Read-Only Memory
FAQ	Frequently Asked Questions
FAX	Facsimile
FDDI	Fibre Distributed Data Interface
FIFO	First In, First Out
Fortran	Formula Translation
FTP	File Transfer Protocol
GIF	Graphics Information File
GIGO	Garbage In, Garbage Out
GNU	Gnu's Not Unix
GPS	Global Positioning System
GSM	Global System for Mobile
GUI	Graphical User Interface
HTML	Hypertext Mark-up Language
IBM	International Business Machines
IO	Input-Output
IP	Internet Protocol
ISA	Industry Standard Architecture
ISDN	Integrated Services Digital Network
ISO	International Standards Organisation
JANET	Joint Academic Network
JCL	Job Control Language
JPEG	Joint Picture Experts Group
K	Kilo
LAN	Local Area Network
LED	Light Emitting Diode
LIFO	Last In, Last Out
LISP	List Processing
M	Mega

MIDI	Musical Instrument Digital Interface
MIMD	Multiple Instructions, Multiple Data
MIME	Multipurpose Internet Mailing Extensions
MIPS	Millions of Instructions Per Second
Modem	Modulator-Demodulator
MOO	MUD, Object Oriented
MRP	Materials Requirements Planning
MUD	Multi-User Dungeon
NACK	Negative Acknowledgement
NNTP	Net News Transfer Protocol
OLE	Object Linking and Embedding
PABX	Private Automatic Branch Exchange
PAL	Phase Alteration by Line
PC	Personal Computer
PCI	Peripheral Components Interface
PCMCIA	Personal Computer Memory Card International Association
PCN	Personal Communications Network
PDA	Personal Digital Assistant
PGP	Pretty Good Privacy
Pixel	Picture Element
POP	Post Office Protocol
POTS	Plain Old Telephone Service
PPP	Point to Point Protocol
PROM	Programmable, Read-Only Memory
PSTN	Public Switched Telephone Network
PTT	Post, Telephone and Telegraph
RAID	Redundant Array of Inexpensive Disks
RAM	Random Access Memory
RISC	Reduced Instruction Set Computing
ROM	Read-Only Memory
RTF	Rich Text Format
SCSI	Small Computer Systems Interface
SECAM	Séquence Couleur A Mémoire
SGML	Standard Generalised Mark-up Language
SIMD	Single Instruction, Multiple Data
SIMM	Single In-line Memory Module

SLIP	Serial Line Interface Protocol
SMTP	Simple Mail Transfer Protocol
SNA	Systems Network Architecture
SNMP	Simple Net Management Protocol
SQL	Structured Query Language
SRAM	Static Random Access Memory
TCP/IP	Transfer Control Protocol/Internet Protocol
TDMA	Time Division Multiple Access
TIFF	Tagged Image File Format
TLA	Three Letter Acronym
TTY	Teletype
TWAIN	Tool Without an Interesting Name
UART	Universal Asynchronous Receiver/Transmitter
URL	Universal Resource Locator
UUCP	Unix to Unix Copy Protocol
VMS	Vax proprietary operating system
VRAM	Video Random Access Memory
VSAT	Very Small Aperture Satellite
WAIS	Wide Area Information Service
WAN	Wide Area Network
WORM	Write Once, Ready Many
WWW	World Wide Web
YMMV	Your Mileage May Vary

2 World's largest IT suppliers, 1993

Rank	Company	IT revenues, $ bn
1	IBM	62,716
2	Fujitsu	21,872
3	NEC	16,675
4	Hewlett Packard	15,600
5	Digital Equipment	13,637
6	Hitachi	12,629
7	AT&T	9,860
8	Toshiba	8,820
9	EDS	8,507
10	Apple	7,900

Source: Datamation.

3 Worldwide PC shipments

Year	Units, '000
1980	609
1981	1,631
1982	4,893
1983	11,123
1984	15,044
1985	14,705
1986	15,064
1987	16,676
1988	18,061
1989	21,327
1990	23,738
1991	27,265
1992	32,407
1993	38,843
1994	47,900

Source: Dataquest.

4 Workstation price/performance

Year	$'000/MIPS
1986	14.60
1987	8.40
1988	5.20
1989	3.00
1990	1.70
1991	1.10
1992	0.70
1993	0.40
1994	0.30
1995	0.20

Source: Dataquest.

5 DRAM prices

Year	$/megabyte
1974	24,576.00
1975	11,264.00
1976	8,521.73
1977	4,804.99
1978	3,467.58
1979	3,167.21
1980	2,136.62
1981	844.58
1982	599.97
1983	521.95
1984	381.82
1985	89.39
1986	81.26
1987	90.67
1988	125.84
1989	78.70
1990	47.84
1991	32.52
1992	23.44
1993	27.49
1994	26.15

Source: Dataquest.

6 Computers connected to the Internet

Date	No.
Aug 1981	213
May 1982	235
Aug 1983	562
Oct 1984	1,024
Oct 1985	1,961
Feb 1986	2,308
Nov 1986	5,089
Dec 1987	28,174
Jul 1988	33,000
Oct 1988	56,000
Jan 1989	80,000
Jul 1989	130,000
Oct 1989	159,000
Oct 1990	313,000
Jan 1991	376,000
Jul 1991	535,000
Oct 1991	617,000
Jan 1992	727,000
Apr 1992	890,000
Jul 1992	992,000
Oct 1992	1,136,000
Jan 1993	1,313,000
Apr 1993	1,486,000
Jul 1993	1,776,000
Oct 1993	2,056,000
Dec 1993	2,217,000
Jul 1994	3,212,000
Oct 1994	3,864,000
Jan 1995	4,852,000
Apr 1995	5,706,114

Source: Internet Society.

7 Recommended reading

Champy, James and Hammer, Michael, *Re-engineering the Corporation*, HarperCollins, New York, 1993.
Over-optimistic, perhaps, but still the re-engineering Bible.

Forester, Tom (ed.), *Computers in the Human Context*, MIT Press, Cambridge, MA, 1991.
An interesting, if ageing, collection of essays on the social, business and human impact of information technology.

Freiberger, Paul and Swaine, Michael, *Fire in the Valley*, Osborne/McGraw Hill, Berkeley, CA, 1984.
Out of print, but still an excellent history of the invention of the personal computer.

Kelly, Kevin, *Out of Control: The Rise of Neo-Biological Civilization*, Addison-Wesley, Reading, MA, 1994.
An amazing collection of neat stuff, mostly to do with new technology and its impact on life as we know it.

Krol, Ed, *The Whole Internet User's Guide & Catalog*, O'Reilly & Associates, Sebastopol, CA, 1992.
First and probably still the best of the user's guides to the Internet.

Levy, Stephen, *Artificial Life*, Jonathan Cape, London, 1992.
A good, non-technical introduction to the field.

Pool, Ithiel de Sola, *Technologies of Freedom*, Belknap Press, Cambridge, MA, 1983.
Still the classic work on the regulation and politics of new media.

Raymond, Eric, *The New Hacker's Dictionary*, MIT Press, Cambridge, MA, 1991.
How to decode a coder, plus some jokes.